FREE Study Skills DVD (

Dear Customer,

Thank you for your purchase from Mometrix! We consider it an honor and privilege that you have purchased our product and want to ensure your satisfaction.

As a way of showing our appreciation and to help us better serve you, we have developed a Study Skills DVD that we would like to give you for <u>FREE</u>. **This DVD covers our "best practices" for studying for your exam, from using our study materials to preparing for the day of the test.**

All that we ask is that you email us your feedback that would describe your experience so far with our product. Good, bad or indifferent, we want to know what you think!

To get your **FREE Study Skills DVD**, email <u>freedvd@mometrix.com</u> with "FREE STUDY SKILLS DVD" in the subject line and the following information in the body of the email:

    a.   The name of the product you purchased.

    b.   Your product rating on a scale of 1-5, with 5 being the highest rating.

    c.   Your feedback. It can be long, short, or anything in-between, just your impressions and experience so far with our product. Good feedback might include how our study material met your needs and will highlight features of the product that you found helpful.

    d.   Your full name and shipping address where you would like us to send your free DVD.

If you have any questions or concerns, please don't hesitate to contact me directly.

Thanks again!

Sincerely,

Jay Willis
Vice President
<u>jay.willis@mometrix.com</u>
1-800-673-8175

ASWB
Bachelors Exam
SECRETS

Study Guide
Your Key to Exam Success

ASWB Test Review for the
Association of Social Work Boards Exam

Published by
Mometrix Test Preparation
ASWB Exam Secrets Test Prep Team

Written and edited by the ASWB Exam Secrets Test Prep Staff

Printed in the United States of America

This paper meets the requirements of ANSI/NISO Z39.48-1992 (Permanence of Paper).

Mometrix offers volume discount pricing to institutions. For more information or a price quote, please contact our sales department at sales@mometrix.com or 888-248-1219.

Mometrix Media LLC is not affiliated with or endorsed by any official testing organization. All organizational and test names are trademarks of their respective owners.

ISBN 13: 978-1-60971-217-4
ISBN 10: 1-60971-217-X

Dear Future Exam Success Story:

Congratulations on your purchase of our study guide. Our goal in writing our study guide was to cover the content on the test, as well as provide insight into typical test taking mistakes and how to overcome them.

Standardized tests are a key component of being successful, which only increases the importance of doing well in the high-pressure high-stakes environment of test day. How well you do on this test will have a significant impact on your future, and we have the research and practical advice to help you execute on test day.

The product you're reading now is designed to exploit weaknesses in the test itself, and help you avoid the most common errors test takers frequently make.

How to use this study guide

We don't want to waste your time. Our study guide is fast-paced and fluff-free. We suggest going through it a number of times, as repetition is an important part of learning new information and concepts.

First, read through the study guide completely to get a feel for the content and organization. Read the general success strategies first, and then proceed to the content sections. Each tip has been carefully selected for its effectiveness.

Second, read through the study guide again, and take notes in the margins and highlight those sections where you may have a particular weakness.

Finally, bring the manual with you on test day and study it before the exam begins.

Your success is our success

We would be delighted to hear about your success. Send us an email and tell us your story. Thanks for your business and we wish you continued success.

Sincerely,

Mometrix Test Preparation Team

Need more help? Check out our flashcards at: http://MometrixFlashcards.com/ASWB

TABLE OF CONTENTS

Top 20 Test Taking Tips

1. Carefully follow all the test registration procedures
2. Know the test directions, duration, topics, question types, how many questions
3. Setup a flexible study schedule at least 3-4 weeks before test day
4. Study during the time of day you are most alert, relaxed, and stress free
5. Maximize your learning style; visual learner use visual study aids, auditory learner use auditory study aids
6. Focus on your weakest knowledge base
7. Find a study partner to review with and help clarify questions
8. Practice, practice, practice
9. Get a good night's sleep; don't try to cram the night before the test
10. Eat a well balanced meal
11. Know the exact physical location of the testing site; drive the route to the site prior to test day
12. Bring a set of ear plugs; the testing center could be noisy
13. Wear comfortable, loose fitting, layered clothing to the testing center; prepare for it to be either cold or hot during the test
14. Bring at least 2 current forms of ID to the testing center
15. Arrive to the test early; be prepared to wait and be patient
16. Eliminate the obviously wrong answer choices, then guess the first remaining choice
17. Pace yourself; don't rush, but keep working and move on if you get stuck
18. Maintain a positive attitude even if the test is going poorly
19. Keep your first answer unless you are positive it is wrong
20. Check your work, don't make a careless mistake

Human Development, Diversity, and Behavior in the Environment

Kohlberg's theory of moral development

Kohlberg formulated his theory to extend and modify the work of Piaget, as he believed that moral development was a longer and more complex process. He postulated that infants possess no morals or ethics at birth and that moral development occurs largely independently of age. Kohlberg asserted that children's experiences shape their understanding of moral concepts (e.g., justice, rights, equality, human welfare). Kohlberg suggested a process involving three levels, each with two stages. Each stage reveals a dramatic change in the moral perspective of the individual. In this theory, moral development is linear, no stage can be skipped, and development takes place throughout the life span. Progress between stages is contingent upon the availability of a role model who offers a model of the principles of the next higher level.

Stage 1
Stage 1 belongs in the pre-conventional or primitive level. The individual perspective frames moral judgments, which are concrete. The framework of Stage 1 stresses rule following, because breaking rules may lead to punishment. Reasoning in this stage is ego-centric and is not concerned with others.

Stage 2
Stage 2 is the second stage in the pre-conventional level. It emphasizes moral reciprocity and has its focus on the pragmatic, instrumental value of an action. Individuals at this stage observe moral standards because it is in their interest, but they are able to justify retaliation as a form of justice. Behavior in this stage is focused on following rules only when it is in the person's immediate interest. Stage 2 has a mutual contractual nature, which makes rule-following instrumental and based on externalities. There is, however, an understanding of conventional morality.

Stage 3
Stage three is the first stage in the "conventional level." Individuals in Stage 3 define morality in reference to what is expected by those with whom they have close relationships. Emphasis of this stage is on stereotypic roles (good mother, father, sister). Virtue is achieved through maintaining trusting and loyal relationships.

Stage 4
Stage 4 is the second stage in the "conventional level." In this stage, the individual shifts from basically narrow local norms and role expectations to a larger social system perspective. Social responsibilities and observance of laws are key aspects of social responsibility. Individuals in this stage reflect higher levels of abstraction in understanding laws' significance. Individuals at Stage 4 have a sophisticated understanding of the law and only violate laws when they conflict with social duties. Observance of the law is seen as necessary to maintain the protections that the legal system provides to all.

<u>Stages 5 and 6</u>
According to Kohlberg, a minority of people attain the final level, which is "Post-conventional Morality," as only 10-15% of people are capable of the type of abstract thinking necessary for Stages 5 and 6. In Stage 5, the individual becomes aware that while rules and laws exist for the good of the greatest number, there are times when they will work against the interest of particular individuals. Issues may not always be clear cut and the individual may have to decide to disregard some rules or laws in order to uphold a higher good (such as the protection of life).

In Stage 6 individuals have developed their own set of moral guidelines, which may or may not fit with the law. Principles such as human rights, justice, and equality apply to everyone and the individual must be prepared to act to defend these principles, even if it means going against the rest of society and paying the consequences (e.g., disapproval or imprisonment). Kohlberg believed very few, if any, people reached this stage.

Carol Gilligan's Morality of Care

This is the feminist response to Kohlberg's moral development theory. Kohlberg's theory was based on research only on men. Gilligan purports that a morality of care reflects women's experience more accurately than one emphasizing justice and rights. Morality of care reflects caring, responsibility, and non-violence; morality of justice and rights emphasizes equality. The two types of moralities give two distinct charges—to not treat others unfairly (justice/rights) and to not turn away from someone in need (care). Care stresses interconnectedness and nurturing. Emphasizing justice stems from a focus on individualism. Aspects of attachment—Justice/Rights requires individuation and separation from the parent, which leads to awareness of power differences. Care emphasizes a continuing attachment to parent, less awareness of inequalities, not a primary focus on fairness.

Freud's theories

<u>Freud's psychoanalytic theory</u>
These are the three levels of the mind that Freud proposed. The conscious mind is comprised of various ideas and thoughts of which we are fully aware. The preconscious mind is comprised of ideas and thoughts that are outside of immediate awareness, but can be readily accessed and brought into awareness. The unconscious mind is comprised of thoughts and ideas that are outside of our awareness and that cannot be accessed or brought into full awareness by personal effort alone.

<u>Motivational forces of the unconscious mind that shape behavior</u>
Psychoanalytic theory postulates that behavior is influenced not only by environmental stimuli (i.e., physical influences) and external social constrains and constructs (e.g., taboos, rules, social expectations), but also by four specific unconscious elements as well. These elements exist only in the unconscious mind and individuals remain substantively unaware of all the forces, motivations, and drive which shape their thoughts and behavioral decisions. The four elements are as follows:
- Covert desires
- Defenses needed to protect, facilitate, and moderate behaviors
- Dreams
- Unconscious wishes

Freud's psychosexual stages of development

Freud's psychosexual stages of development are as follows:

- Oral stage: birth to 1.5 yrs, gratification through mouth/upper digestive tract
- Anal stage: 1.5-3 yrs, child gains control over anal sphincter and bowel movements
- Phallic stage: 3-5 yrs, gratification through genitalia. Major task is resolution of oedipal complex and leads to development of superego, which begins about age 4. During this time child's phallic striving is directed toward opposite-sex parent and in competition with same-sex parent. Out of fear and love, child renounces desire for opposite sex parent and represses sexual desires. Child then identifies with same-sex parent and internalizes their values, etc. This leads to development of superego and ability to experience guilt.
- Latency stage: 6-10 yrs, sublimation of oedipal stage, expression of sexual-aggressive drives in socially acceptable forms
- Genital stage: 10 yrs to adulthood, acceptance of one's genitalia, concern for others' well being.

Psychoanalysis

The primary focus of psychoanalysis is on the unconscious mind and the desires, defenses, dreams and wishes contained therin. Freud proposed that the key features of the unconscious mind arise from experiences in the past and from problems in the development of the personality. Consequently, a focus on the unconscious mind requires the psychoanalytic process to also focus on the past—specifically on those repressed infanct and childhood memories and experiences which served to create the desires, defenses, dreams, and wishes that invariably become manifest through the thoughts and behaviors of every individual.

Freud's structural theory of personality development

Freud proposed a three-level structure of personality, composed of the id, the ego, and the super-ego. The id is the level of personality that comprises basic instinctual drives and is the only part of personality present at birth. The id seeks immediate gratification of primitive needs (hunger, thirst, libido) and adheres to the "pleasure principle" (i.e. seek pleasure, avoid pain). The ego develops secondarily and allows for rational thought, executive functions, and the ability to delay gratification. The ego is governed by the "reality principle" and mediates the desires of the id with the requirements of the external world. The super-ego develops last and incorporates the higher concepts of morality, ethics, and justice into the personality, allowing concepts of right, wrong, and greater good to override base instincts and purely rational goals.

Adult personality types

Adult personality types according to Sigmund Freud are:

- Oral personality: infantile, demanding, dependent behavior; preoccupation with oral gratification.
- Anal personality: stinginess, excessive focus on accumulating and collecting. Rigidity in routines and forms, suspiciousness, legalistic thinking.
- Phallic personality: selfish sexual exploitation of others, without regard to their needs or concerns.

Processes and stages relevant to personality development

Freud identified two primary elements that contribute to the development of the personality:

- Natural growth and maturational processes (biological, hormonal, time-dependent processes)

- Learning and experiential processes (coping with and avoiding pain, managing frustration, reducing anxiety, and resolving conflicts)

The five developmental stages he identified are:
1. Oral stage
2. Anal stage
3. Phallic stage
4. Latency stage
5. Genital stage

Psychopathology will result if all stages of development are not fully mastered, or if fixation at a particular stage develops (resulting if needs at a particular stage are either over- or under-gratified). If significant developmental frustration is experienced in a later stage, the developmental process may fall back to an earlier stage by means of the defense mechanism known as regression.

Cathexis and anti-cathexis
According to Freud's theory, the individual's mental state emerges from the process of reciprocal exchange between two forces: cathexis and anti-cathexis. Freud used the term cathexis to refer to the psychic energy attached to an object of importance (e.g., person, body part, psychic element). He also used this term to refer to what he called "urges," or psychic impulses such as desires, wishes, pain, etc., that drive human behavior. In contrast to the driving urges of cathexis, there is a checking force he referred to as anti-cathexis. It serves to restrict the urges of the id and also to keep repressed information in the unconscious mind.

Aspects of the super-ego
The super-ego is comprised of the conscience and the ego ideal, which are constructed from the restraints and encouragements provided by caregivers (parents, teachers, other role models). The conscience focuses on cognitive and behavioral restrictions (i.e., the "should nots") while the ego ideal focuses on perfection, including spiritual attainment and higher-order goals (the "shoulds" of thought and behavior). The super-ego works in opposition to the id and produces feelings of guilt for inappropriate drives, fantasies, and actions and encouraging refinement, aspirations, and higher-order goals. Freud theorized that the super-ego emerges around age five, and is not the dominant feature of the personality in a healthy person (which would result in overly-rigid, rule-bound behavior). The strongest part of the personality is the ego, which seeks to satisfy the needs of the id without disrupting the super-ego.

Piaget's theory of cognitive and moral development

Piaget theorized that all human development and behavior arises from interactive patterns or templates he called *schemas*. These are the cognitive constructs through which one explores and learns about the physical and social world. Schemas are goal-oriented systems of mental organization that are both sensorimotor (based in movement and sensation) and cognitive (based in perception and experience). According to Piaget, learning occurs via adaptation, a two-part process consisting of assimilation (integration of perceptions into a schema) and accommodation (modifying a schema to fit a new object, experience, or situation). Piaget believed that a child's processes of cognitive development can be categorized into four hierarchical stages:
1. Sensorimotor
2. Preoperational
3. Concrete operational
4. Formal operational.

Sensorimotor stage

The sensorimotor stage begins at birth and lasts through about two years of age. During this stage, an infant explores the world using motor functions and sensoria. The sucking reflex plays a prominent role in this stage (i.e., nursing). During this stage early circular interactive patterns emerge—for example thumb-sucking is pleasant, the pleasure reinforces the behavior. During the sensorimotor stage an infant is not able to utilize symbolic representation. For example, the infant is unable relate to people or objects when they are absent.

Preoperational stage

The preoperational stage in Piaget's theory of development begins around age 2 and lasts through about age 7. During this stage, a child develops the capacity for symbolism, which is evident through drawing, language, and speech. Children in the preoperational stage become increasingly cognizant of the concepts of past and future. An example of this is seen in the ability to soothe a crying child by reassuring her "We'll be going home soon." A self-centered focus predominates during this period.

Concrete operational stage

The concrete operational stage of development begins around age seven and lasts through about age eleven. During this stage, a child develops the capacity to manipulate symbols in a logical fashion. For example, whether you stack two items or place them in a row, a child in the concrete operational stage will be able to indicate that there are only two items involved. During this stage, a child comes to understand the principle of conservation of substance. When a liquid is poured from a pitcher into four glasses, the child will be able to understand that the total amount of liquid remains the same.

Formal operational stage

The final stage in Piaget's theory of development is the formal operational stage. This stage begins around age eleven and extends through about age fifteen. During the formal operational stage, a child is able to begin cognitively perceiving and analyzing his or her world in adult ways. Logical operations move from being solely concrete in nature to encompass abstract thinking. The concept of hypothetical thinking (also called abstract thinking) is developed during this stage.

Action, operation, activity in development, accommodation, and assimilation

The following are terms according to the work of Piaget:

- Action - overt behavior
- Operation - a particular type of action; may be internalized thought
- Activity in Development - the child is not a passive subject, but rather an active contributor to the construction of his or her personality and universe. The child acts on his or her environment, modifies it, and is an active participant in the construction of reality.
- Accommodation - type of adaptation which entails adapting to the characteristics of the object
- Assimilation - type of adaptation which incorporates external reality into the existing mental organization

Erik Erikson's psychosocial theory

Erikson's psychosocial theory has roots in Freud's psychoanalytic theory. Erikson accepts Freud's belief that childhood experiences shape much of personality. He proposed that personality development continued past the age of 5. Psychosocial theory emphasizes the capacity for personality growth and change, in comparison with the psychoanalytic view, which takes a more deterministic view of personality. The foundation of psychosocial theory is that all individuals have innate value and the capacity to learn and adapt and to influence their environment both socially and physically. Biological and social system influences are acknowledged, though the psychosocial system is seen as paramount in determining behavior. The individual develops after passing through eight well-defined stages, each of which demonstrates a unique combination of needs and vulnerabilities. Each stage has its focus on some aspect of growth and culminates in an encounter or crisis. The outcome of the encounter or crisis leads to the development of an important human quality.

Erikson was one of the first theorists to address human development over the entire life span. The eight developmental stages in this theory are:
1. Trust vs. Mistrust
2. Autonomy vs. Shame
3. Initiative vs. Guilt
4. Industry vs. Inferiority
5. Identity vs. Role confusion
6. Intimacy vs. Isolation
7. Generativity vs. Stagnation
8. Ego integrity vs. Despair

The stages are hierarchical and build upon each other. The resolution of the fundamental "crisis" of each prior stage must occur before one can move on to the next stage of growth. Although individual attributes are primary in resolving the crisis associated with each stage, the social environment can play an important role as well.

The psychosocial stages are summarized below:
- Trust vs. Mistrust
    - Takes place between birth to 1.5 years old
    - In this stage, infants develop a sense of trust in self and in others.
    - Psychological dangers include a strong mistrust that later develops and is revealed as withdrawal when the individual is at odds with self and others.
- Autonomy vs. Shame and Doubt
    - Takes place between 1.5 to 3 years old. Covers same ages as Freud's Anal Stage.
    - In this phase, rapid growth in muscular maturation, verbalization, and the ability to coordinate highly conflicting action patterns is characterized by tendencies of holding on and letting go.
    - The child begins experiencing an autonomous will, which contributes to the process of identity building and development of the courage to be an independent individual.
    - Psychological dangers include immature obsessiveness and procrastination, ritualistic repetitions to gain power, self-insistent stubbornness, compulsive meek compliance or self-restraint, and the fear of a loss of self-control.
- Initiative vs. Guilt
    - Takes place between 3-6 years old. Covers same ages as Freud's Phallic Stage.
    - Incursion into space by mobility, into the unknown by curiosity, and into others by physical attack and aggressive voice.
    - This stage frees the child's initiative and sense of purpose for adult tasks.
    - Psychological dangers include hysterical denial or self-restriction, which impede an individual from actualizing inner capacities.

- Industry vs. Inferiority
  - Takes place between ages 6-11 years old and corresponds to Freud's Latency Stage.
  - The need of the child is to make things well, to be a worker and a potential provider.
  - Developmental task is mastery over physical objects, self, social transaction, ideas, and concepts.
  - School and peer groups are necessary for gaining and testing mastery.
  - Psychological dangers include a sense of inferiority, incompetence, self-restraint, and conformity.
- Identity vs. Role Confusion
  - Takes place during adolescence and corresponds with Freud's Genital Stage.
  - Crucial task is to create an identity, reintegration of various components of self into a whole person—a process of ego synthesis.
  - The peer group is greatly important in providing support, values, a primary reference group, and an arena in which to experiment with various roles.
  - Psychological dangers include extreme identity confusion, feelings of estrangement, excessive conformity or rebelliousness, and idealism (a denial of reality, neurotic conflict, or delinquency).
- Intimacy vs. Isolation
  - Takes place in early adulthood.
  - Major task is to enter relationships with others in an involved, reciprocal manner.
  - Failure to achieve intimacy can lead to highly stereotyped interpersonal relationships and distancing. Can also lead to a willingness to renounce, isolate, and destroy others whose presence seems dangerous.
- Generativity vs. Stagnation
  - Takes place in middle adulthood.
  - The key task is to develop concern for establishing and guiding the next generation, and the capacity for caring, nurturing, and concern for others.
  - Psychological danger is stagnation. Stagnation includes caring primarily for oneself, an artificial intimacy with others, and self-indulgence.
- Integrity vs. Despair
  - Takes place in later adulthood.
  - Primary task is the acceptance of one's life, achievements, and significant relationships as satisfactory and acceptable.
  - Psychological danger is despair. Despair is expressed in having the sense that time is too short to start another life or to test alternative roads to integrity.
  - Despair is accompanied by self-criticism, regret, and fear of impending death.

Executive function

Executive functions are cognitive features that control and regulate all other abilities and behaviors. These are higher-level abilities that influence attention, memory, and motor skills. They also monitor actions and providet he capacity to initiate, stop, or change behaviors, to set goals and plan future behavior, and to solve problems when faced with complex tasks and situations. Executive functions allow one to form concepts and think abstractly. Deficits in executive functioning is evident in the reduced ability to delay gratification, problems udnerstanding cause and effect (i.e., concrete thinking), poor organization and planning, difficulty following multi-step directions, perseveration with an idea in the face of superior information, and overall poor judgment.

Defense mechanisms

According to Anna Freud, defense mechanisms are an unconscious process in which the ego attempts to expel anxiety-provoking sexual and aggressive impulses from consciousness. Defense mechanisms are attempts to protect the self from painful anxiety and are used universally. In themselves they are not an indication of pathology, but rather an indication of disturbance when their cost outweighs their protective value. Anna Freud proposed that defense mechanisms serve to protect the ego and to reduce angst, fear, and distress through irrational distortion, denial, and/or obscuring reality. Defense mechanisms are deployed when the ego senses the threat of harm from thoughts or acts incongruent with rational behavior or conduct demanded by the super-ego. The following are important terms associated with defense mechanisms:

- Compensation - protection against feelings of inferiority and inadequacy stemming from real or imagined personal defects or weaknesses
- Conversion - somatic changes conveyed in symbolic body language; psychic pain is felt in a part of the body
- Denial - avoidance of awareness of some painful aspect of reality
- Displacement - investing repressed feelings in a substitute object
- Association - altruism; acquiring gratification through connection with and helping another person who is satisfying the same instincts.
- Identification - manner by which one becomes like another person in one or more respects. It is a more elaborate process than introjection.
- Introjection - absorbing an idea or image so that it becomes part of oneself.
- Inversion - turning against the self. The object of aggressive drive is changed from another to the self-especially in depression and masochism.
- Isolation - of affect separation of ideas from the feelings originally associated with them. Remaining idea is deprived of motivational force; action is impeded and guilt avoided.
- Intellectualization - psychological binding of instinctual drives in intellectual activities, for example the adolescent's preoccupation with philosophy and religion.
- Projection - ascribing a painful idea or impulse to the external world
- Rationalization - effort to give a logical explanation for painful unconscious material to avoid guilt and shame.
- Reaction formation - replacing in conscious awareness a painful idea or feeling with its opposite
- Regression - withdrawal to an earlier phase of psychosexual development
- Repression - the act of obliterating material from conscious awareness. Is capable of mastering powerful impulses.
- Reversal - type of reaction formation aimed at protection from painful thoughts/feelings
- Splitting - seeing external objects as either all good or all bad. Feelings may rapidly shift from one category to the other.
- Sublimation - redirecting energies of instinctual drives to generally positive goals that are more acceptable to the ego and superego.
- Substitution - trading of one affect for another (e.g., rage masking fear)
- Undoing - ritualistically performing the opposite of an act one has recently carried out in order to cancel out or balance the evil that may have been present in the act
- Identification with the Aggressor - a child's introjections of some characteristic of an anxiety evoking object and assimilation of an anxiety experience just lived through. In this, the child can transform from the threatened person into the one making the threat.

Alfred Adler's cognitive theory

Adler is the founder of individual psychology and took a holistic approach to psychology. His cognitive approach incorporates psychodynamic, cognitive behavioral, existential, and humanistic principles. It differs from Freud's psychoanalytic approach in three key ways:
1. The personality is not subdivided but must be viewed as a whole
2. Social motivation, not sexual drive, guides behavior

Conscious thoughts and beliefs are paramount, as opposed to Freud's focus on the unconscious, though unconscious misconceptions, false beliefs and irrational thoughts do exert influence. Physiological, neurological, and chemical problems can also shape behavior.

Albert Ellis' cognitive theory

Ellis founded the cognitive theory known as Rational Emotive Therapy (RET), also referred to as the "ABC theory of emotion." This theory holds that rational thought produces psychological health. Using the ABC model, the A refers to any activating event, B refers to beliefs about A, and C refers to the consequences (emotional and behavioral). Rational thought ensures functional beliefs and successful consequences.

Behavioral theory

Behavioral theory proposes that all behaviors are learned in one way or another; thus, all behaviors can be "unlearned" or changed. The two fundamental theories supporting behavioral theory are 1) classical conditioning (also called respondent conditioning) or the way in which behavior is learned and reinforced by a process of positive association; and 2) operant conditioning, the way in which behaviors are learned by way of positive or negative reinforcement. The earliest theorists responsible for formulating classical conditioning were John Watson and Ivan Pavlov, while operant conditioning was developed by B. F. Skinner.

Social learning theory

Social learning theory proposes that all behaviors are learned, as in behavioral theory. Social learning theory, however, focuses on altering the events before and after a target behavior to bring about change. A primary proponent of social learning theory was Albert Bandura, who stated that behavior is learned from the environment through the process of observational learning. Social learning theory has three specific components that are used to shape behavior: the antecedent event (some environmental event which arises before the target behavior, the target behavior (the act to be changed, and the consequence (an outcome of the behavior). Manipulation of the antecedent event and/or the consequence will result in altered behavior (e.g., ignoring rather than reacting to a tantrum) and will eventually extinguish it.

Operant conditioning

Operant conditioning involves changes in the environment coupled with reinforcement by significant others, resulting in behavioral change. "Reinforcement" is the process by which positive or negative stimuli result in increased or decreased behavior. Positive reinforcement can be any of a variety of rewards, such as praise, treats, privileges, or something else. Negative reinforcement uses aversive events or items (i.e., anything undesirable). This causes a specific behavior to avoid or escape the negative reinforcer. Punishment is not the same as negative reinforcement. Negative reinforcement is used to increase a target behvior, while punishment is designed to decrease a target behavior.

Classical conditioning

Classical (or respondent) conditioning produces behavior by means of association, such as pairing a positive stimulus with a neutral stimulus to produce a behavior. The behavior elicited (or a "conditioned response") can either be emitted (voluntary) or reflexive (involuntary). Ivan Pavlov demonstrated this with his famous study of dog salivation, wherein food was presented to dogs with the ringing of a bell. Food was the unconditioned stimulus, and salivation at seeing food was the unconditioned response. Eventually the dogs salivated at the sound of the bell absent any food. Thus, the bell became the conditioned stimulus, and salivation became the conditioned response. Similarly, John B. Watson was famous for his "Little Albert" experiment, which produced a conditioned response in a child. The child was given a white rat to play with, and Watson would produce a loud clanging noise behind the child whenever he engaged the rat. Eventually the child became terrified at the sight of the rat.

B. F. Skinner

Skinner develped the Empty Organism Concept, which proposes that an infant has the capacity for action built into his or her physical makeup. The infant also has reflexes and motivation that will set this capacity in random motion. Skinner asserted that the Law of Effect governs development. Behavior of children is shaped largely by adults. Behaviors that result in satisfying consequences are likely to be repeated under similar circumstances. Halting or discontinuing behavior is accomplished by denying satisfying rewards or through punishment. Skinner also theorized about Schedules of Reinforcement—rather than reinforceing every instance of a correct response, one can reinforce a fixed percentage of correct responses, or space reinforcements according to some interval of time. Intermittet reinforcement will reinforce the desired behavior.

Systematic Desensitization and Flooding

Systematic desensitization is a therapy used to treat anxiety disorders, typically those caused by a specific stimulus. The patient is progressively exposed to anxiety-inducing objects, images, or situations, or is asked to imagine them, and is then encouraged to practice relaxation or other coping techniques to manage or eliminate the anxiety. Once the client learns to cope with a given level of exposure, the intensity of the exposure is increased and the process is repeated. This continues until the client is successfully desensitized to the stimulus. Flooding is an extreme form of desensitization by exposure. While typical systematic desensitization gradually increases the intensity of the stimulus, flooding jumps directly to the final stage. The client is subjected to the full intensity of the anxiety-inducing stimulus for a prolonged period of time, sometimes several hours. Part of the reasoning for this method is that all of the physiology-based fear responses can only affect the person for limited time, and once the client is no longer affected, they will be better able to train themselves not to fear the stimulus.

Theory of Cultural Relativism

Values, beliefs, models of behavior, and understandings of the nature of the universe must be understood within the cultural framework in which they appear. The outlines and limitations of normality and deviance are determined by the dominant culture. Ethnic/minority behavioral norms and expressions of emotional needs may be defined as abnormal in that they differ from those of the larger, dominant culture. Behaviors and attitudes may be perceived differently If understood through a unique cultural context. It is important for a worker to know whether a client from a particular ethnic group who displays unorthodox behavior is also deviant within his or her own culture, as well as in his or her self-assessment.

Heinz Hartmann's ego psychology

Ego psychology was derived from psychoanalytic theory and focuses on the ego in Freud's theory of personality. Central tenets include the following:
1. Everyone is born with the capacity to adapt to social environments, as both the id and the ego are present at birth (contrary to Freud's belief that only the id is present at birth.
2. The ego is primarily responsible for adaptation.
3. Adaptation requires ego-based choices.
4. Adaptation occurs via alloplastic behavior (adaptive changes to the environment) or autoplastic behavior (adaptive changes to the self).

Successful adaptation is accomplished by way of 12 major ego functions, which facilitate the change and adaptation process in social environments. Hartmann's 12 ego functions include:
1. Reality sensation, the capacity to both perceive and experience things in the environment accurately.
2. Reality testing, the capacity to differentiate and make accurate observations regarding the self and the environment.
3. Judgment, the capacity to identify a behavior and sucessfully weigh the consequences of carrying it out prior to taking any action.
4. Drive and impulse control, the capacity to regulate drives and impulses in concert with reality.
5. Object relations, the capacity to relate to and interact with others.
6. Controlled thought processes, the capacity to organize and direct thoughts toward realistic ends and goals.
7. Adaptive regression, the capacity to suspend reality in order to experience portions of the self that would not otherwise be accessible
8. Defensive functioning, the capacity to reduce anxiety and mitigate otherwise painful experiences by means of unconscious self-preservation mechanisms
9. Stimulus barrier, the capacity to accommodate increases and decreases in environment stimulation sufficient to maintain the current level of functioning.
10. Autonomous functions, the capacity for essential conflict-free functions to occur independently and concurrently, such as concentration, learning, memory, and perception.
11. Mastery-competence, the capacity to engage the environment successfully.
12. Integrative functioning, the capacity to resolve conflict by integrating certain parts of the personality.

Margaret Mahler's object relations theory

Margaret Mahler's object relations theory is another offshoot of psychoanalytic theory. The emphasis is on interpersonal relationships, particularly between mother and child. An "object" is something to which one relates—usually persons, parts of persons, or symbols of one of these. Key concepts include:
1. The drive to understand the self and others is present from birth.
2. The drive to build interpersonal relationships is present at birth.

3. All interpersonal relationships are affected by the quality of an individual's understanding of self and others.
4. Residues of past relations affect a person in the present.
5. During the first 3½ years of life, a child learns to differentiate between the self and others.
6. Object relations arise through a child's ego organization during the first 3½ years of life.

Mahler's three stages of development are:
1. The "autistic" stage (newborn to 1 month), in which there is total focus on self and obliviousness to external stimuli.
2. The "symbiotic" stage (1-5 months after birth), in which the "need satisfying object" (caregiver) begins to be identified as such and gradually as separate from the self.
3. The "separation-individuation" stage (5 months to 2 years and beyond), which consists of four substages:
   a. Differentiation (5-9 months), the shift to an outward focus and early separation from the caregiver.
   b. Practicing (9-14 months), in which autonomous ego functions begin to emerge, along with increasing mobility.
   c. Rapprochement (14-24 months), in which the child moves away from the caregiver, but with regular returns.
   d. Object constancy (after 24 months), in which the caregiver relationship becomes internalized, with the child recognizing her continued existence even when she is absent.

Gestalt psychology

As suggested by the name *Gestalt* (a derivative of the German word for wholeness), this theoretical approach focuses on the individual from a holistic perspective. Although Gestalt theory recognizes the role of unconscious drives, it opts to focus primarily on the "here and now" rather than the influences of the past. Even so, many issues and problems are seen as rooted in past experiences (both relational and environmental). However, immediate behaviors are perceived as fully conscious choices that are entirely in the individual's control, along with the power to change. This theory does not subscribe to any discrete, multi-stage process of personal development. Instead, it sees development as a process unique to each individual. Rather than focusing on personality as an aggregation of parts, it is seen as parts integrated into a whole.

Heinz Kohut's self-psychology

Psychoanalytic self-psychology rejects Freud's primary focus on the sexual drives in the organization of the human psyche, as instinctual drives are not seen as integral to the development of a cohesive self. The role of empathy is seen as crucial in human development, with nurturing "selfobjects" seen as paramount (as people and objects are perceived by the infant as part of the self). The primary selfobject (mother) attends to the child by way of "empathic mirroring" (hearing and responding to the child's needs), which ultimately helps the child to develop a cohesive self-identity. Thus, self-psychology sees the self/selfobject relationship as the primary focus, as opposed to the self-object relationship of object relations theory. The cohesive self is attained through "transmuting internalization," by which positive, healthy objects are incorporated into the self-structure. Kohut saw narcissism as a normal and integral part of development. Abnormal narcissism occurs only when an empathic environment is lacking, enabling the child unable to transform early grandiose self-images into a more realistic self.

Client population

A client population is the group that is served by an agency, program, or an individual worker. It can also refer to all clients served by all fields of social work. Client population can be defined by age, race, socio-economic status, education level, diagnosis, or any number of characteristics or conditions. A client population can have a very narrow or very broad focus (e.g., all teenagers in a specific geographic area between the ages of 13 and 19, or black men in their twenties who are the first in their families to go to college).

Challenges faced by children in the welfare system

The following are some challenges that children in the child welfare system face in this country:
- Children in foster care often experience frequent relocations for a variety of reasons, including changes in the family situation, decisions made by the court, and rejection by foster families. These frequent changes can cause children in foster care to have to change schools multiple times, which can have an adverse impact on their academic achievement.
- Many foster children experience sexual and physical abuse within the foster care system.
- Many youth "age out" of the foster care system at age 18 (sometimes 21). This can abruptly end the relationships with foster families and other supportive structures (including health care).
- Compared with children raised within their own families, children who have been through the foster care system have a higher incidence of behavioral problems, increased substance abuse, and a greater probability of entering the criminal justice system.

Statistics regarding children in poverty

Some important facts and statistics that deal with children in poverty in the U.S. are as follows:
- Almost one in four children under age six lives in poverty.
- Minority children under age six are much more likely than white children of the same age to live in poverty.
- Many of these children in poverty are homeless or are in the child welfare system
- Fewer than one-third of all poor children below age six live solely on welfare.
- More than half of children in poverty have at least one working parent.
- Children of single mothers are more likely to live in poverty.
- Poor children have increased risk of health impairment.

Racism

Racism can be explained as follows:
- Generalizations, institutionalization, and assignment of values to real or imaginary differences between individuals to justify privilege, aggression, or violence.
- Societal patterns that have the cumulative effect of inflicting oppressive or other negative conditions against identifiable groups based on race or ethnicity.
- Is pervasive, ubiquitous, and institutionalized.

Privilege and oppressed minority

Privilege describes advantages or benefits that the dominant group has that have been given unintentionally, unconsciously, and automatically. An oppressed minority is a group differentiated from others in society because of physical or cultural characteristics. This group receives unequal treatment and views itself as an object of collective discrimination.

Ageism and stereotypes of older adults

Ageism is an attitude toward the capabilities and experiences of old age which leads to devaluation and disenfranchisement. Some common stereotypes of older adults include the following:
- Asexual
- Rigid
- Impaired psychological functioning
- Incapable of change

Culturally sensitive practice

Individual social workers
Culturally sensitive practice describes an ability to work skillfully with cultural differences. It includes the following:
- Awareness and acceptance of differences
- Awareness of one's own cultural values.
- Understanding the dynamics of difference
- Development of cultural knowledge
- An ability to adapt practice skills to fit the cultural context of the client's structure, values, and service.

Cultural sensitivity is an ongoing process that requires continuing education, awareness, management of transference/ counter-transference, and continuious skill development.

Institutions
Cultural sensitivity includes practice skills, attitudes, policies, and structures that are united in a system, in an agency, or among professionals and allow that system, agency or group of professionals to work with cultural differences. It both values diversity (i.e., diverse staff, policies that acknowledge and respect differences, and regular initiation of cultural self assessment) and institutionalizes diversity (i.e., the organization has integrated diversity into its structure, policies, and operations).

Limitations
Some cultural differences may be damaging or unacceptable. The worker needs to have a balanced approach to assess cultural norms within the context of American practices, norms, and laws. There are illegal and unacceptable cultural practices. These may include:
- Child labor
- Honor killings
- Private/family vengeance
- Slavery
- Infanticide
- Female genital mutilation
- Wife or servant beating
- Polygamy
- Child marriage
- Denial of medical care

- Abandonment of disabled children
- Extreme discipline of children

Key assumptions
Key assumptions that underlie culturally-sensitive social work practice are as follows:
- The history of the individual affects the perception, idea generation, and solution of problems.
- The effect of culture on the here-and-now (i.e., the immediate present) is most important.
- Individual behaviors can be affected by unconscious phenomena (often based in culture).
- Influences of cohesion, identity, and strength make up the lived meaning of culture, which may also cause strain and discordance. A meaningful understanding of a client's culture and its immediate impact on the client's life can be essential to addressing any given problem or issue.

Cultural sensitivity

Characteristics
The following are some characteristics of the culturally sensitive social worker:
- With regard for individuality and confidentiality he or she approaches clients in a respectful, warm, accepting, interested manner.
- He or she understands that opinions and experiences of both worker and client are affected by stereotypes and previous experience.
- Is able to acknowledge his or her own socialization to beliefs, attitudes, biases, and prejudices that may affect the working relationship.
- Displays awareness of cross-cultural factors that may affect the relationship.
- Able to communicate that cultural differences and their expressions are legitimate.
- Is open to help from the client in learning about client's background.
- Informed about life conditions fostered by poverty, racism, and disenfranchisement.
- Is aware that client's cultural background may be peripheral to the client's situation and not central to it.

Interpersonal communication
Interpersonal communication is shaped by both culture and context. According to Hall's theory of communication, high context communication styles are used in Asian, Latino, Black, and Native American cultures in the U.S. In this style, there is a strong reliance on contextual cues and a flexible sense of time. This style is intuitive, and within it social roles shape interactions, communication is more personal and affective, and oral agreements are binding. According to Hall's theory, low context communication styles are used more in Northern European, white groups in the U.S. These styles tend to be formal and have complex codes. They tend to show a disregard for contextual codes and a reliance on verbal communication. In these styles, there is an inflexible sense of time. In them, relationships are functionally based, they are highly procedural, and linear logic is used. The worker should be aware of the potential for cross-cultural misunderstanding and that all cultures exhibit great diversity within themselves.

Use of language and communication to become culturally sensitive
A worker can use language and communication in the following ways to become more culturally sensitive:
- Learn to speak the target language.
- Use interpreters appropriately.

- Participate in cultural events of the group(s).
- Form friendships with members of different cultural groups than one's own.
- Acquire cultural and historical information about cultural groups.
- Learn about the institutional barriers that limit access to cultural and economic resources for vulnerable groups.
- Gain an understanding of the socio-political system in the U.S. and the implications for majority and minority groups.

Cultural competence

The following can be done for a social worker to acquire more knowledge in order to become more culturally competent:
- Read applicable practice or scientific professional literature.
- Become familiear with the literature of the relevat group(s).
- Identify and consult with cultural brokers.
- Seek out experiences to interact with diverse groups.

Learn about yourself and your own culture and how it affects your way of thinking and moving in the world. Become aware of your own biases and seek to be open to differences in other cultures.

Standards
The following are ten standards for cultural competence in social work practice:
1. Ethics and values: know relevant standards in the profession and incorporate them into practice
2. Self-Awareness: obtain a greater insight into one's own beliefs and culture, by which to better appreciate diversity in others'.
3. Cross-cultural knowledge: develop the knowledge and insight into other cultures in order to better meet their needs.
4. Cross-cultural skills: develop the skills needed to work with diverse clients.
5. Service delivery: obtain enhanced knowledge of culturally diverse resources for better referrals.
6. Empowerment and advocacy: Become aware of the impact of policies and programs on diverse clients, and advocate for those clients.
7. Diverse Workforce: recruit, hire and retain culturally diverse employees.
8. Professional education: attend educational events to advance cultural competence.
9. Language diversity: provide information and services in the client's language
10. Cross-cultural leadership: Share insights regarding diverse clients with other professionals to advance understanding.

Stages of development
The stages of development of cultural competency in organizations are:
1. Cultural destructiveness (devaluing different cultures and viewing them as inferior)
2. Cultural incapacity (aware of need, feels incapable of providing services—immobility)
3. Cultural blindness ("colorblind," lack of recognition between cultural groups, denial of oppression and institutional racism)
4. Cultural pre-competency (starting to recognize needs of different groups, seeking to recruit diverse staff and include appropriate training)
5. Cultural competency (addresses diversity issues with staff and clients; staff is trained and confident with a range of differences)

6. Cultural proficiency (ideal; ability to incorporate and respond to new cultural groups)

<u>Measures</u>
The following are measures of cultural competence:
- Recognizing effects of cultural differences on the helping process.
- Fully acknowledging one's own culture and its impact on one's thought and action.
- Comprehending the dynamics of power differences in social work practice.
- Comprehending the meaning of a client's behavior in its cultural context.
- Knowing when, where, and how to obtain necessary cultural information.

Barriers to cross-cultural practice

Some barriers to cross-cultural practice are:
- Cultual encapsulation (ethnocentrism, color-blindness, false universals)
- Language barriers (verbal, non-verbal, body language, dialect)
- Class-bound values (treatment, service delivery, power dynamics)
- Culture-bound values

Stresses of immigration

The following are some stresses associated with immigration:
- Gaining entry into and understanding a foreign culture.
- Difficulties with language acquisition.
- Immigrants who are educated often cannot find equivalent employment.
- Distance from family, friends, and familiar surroundings.

Practice issues when working with gay, lesbian, bisexual, or transgender clients

The following are some practice issues when working with clients who may be gay, lesbian, bisexual, or transgender:
- Stigmatization and violence
- Internalized homophobia
- Coming out
- AIDS
- Limited civil rights
- Orientation vs. preference (biology vs. choice)

Community organization practice

<u>Assumptions</u>
The following assumptions underlie community organization practice:
- Members of the community want to improve their situation.
- Members of the community are able to develop the ability to resolve communal and social problems.
- Community members must participate in change efforts rather than have changes imposed on them.
- A systems approach, which considers the total community, is more effective than imposing programs on the community.

- One goal of participation in community organization initiatives involving social workers is education in democratic decision-making and promoting skills for democratic participation.
- The organizer enables members to address community problems independently, in part through their learning, analytic, strategic, and interpersonal skills.

<u>Models</u>
The following are some different models of community organization practice:
- Locality Development
- Social Planning
- Social Action
- Social Reform

Important terms

Acculturation — Acculturation is the process of learning and adopting the dominant culture through adaptation and assimilation.

Ethnic identity — Ethnic identity is a sense of belonging to an identifiable group and having historical continuity, in addition to a sense of common customs and mores transmitted over generations.

Social identity — Social identity describes how the dominant culture establishes criteria for categorizing individuals and the normal and ordinary characteristics believed to be natural and usual for members of the society

Virtual social identity — Virtual social identity is the set of attributes ascribed to persons based on appearances, dialect, social setting, and material features.

Actual social identity — Actual social identity is the set of characteristics a person actually demonstrates.

Stigma — Stigma is a characteristic that makes an individual different from the group and is perceived to be an intensely discreditable trait.

Normification — Normification is an attempt of the stigmatized person to present him or herself as a part of the larger group.

Normalization —Normalization describes trating the stigmatized person as if he or she does not have a stigma.

Culture — Culture describes integrated patterns of human behaviors that include thought, communication, actions, customs, beliefs values, and institutions of a racial ethnic, religious or social group.

Ethnicity — Ethnicity is a group classification in which members share a unique social and cultural heritage that is passed on from one generation to the next. It is not the same as race, though the two terms are sometimes used interchangeably.

Diversity — Diversity refers to the inclusion of social groups that are not easily subsumed into the larger culture. These groups may differ by socioeconomic status, gender, sexual orientation, age, and differential ability.

Socio-economic status — Socio-economic status is the social standing or class of an individual or group. It is determined by occupation, education, and income and can reveal inequities in access to resources, and can highlight issues of privilege, power, and control.

Race — Race can be defined as a subgroup that possesses a definite combination of physical characteristics of a genetic origin. It has no actual biological significance, but does have great social and political significance.

World view — World view describes the way that individuals perceive their relationship to nature, institutions, other people, and objects (i.e., the larger world). This comprises a psychological orientation to life as seen in how individuals think, behave, make decisions, and understand phenomena. It can provide crucial information in assessment.

Prejudice — Prejudice is bias or judgment based on value judgment, personal history, inferences about others, and application of normative judgments.

Discrimination — Discrimination is the act of expressing prejudice with immeiate and serious social and economic consequences.

Stereotyping — Stereotyping describes amplified distorted belief about an ethnic, gender, or other group in order to justify discriminatory conduct.

Assessment

Diagnostic and Statistical Manual of Mental Disorders or DSM

The DSM is now in the fifth version, or the DSM-5. The DSM-5:
- Is a manual which provides a common language and standard criteria for the classification of mental disorders.
- Is a classification system with periodic revisions.
- Includes comprehensive descriptions of the symptoms and manifestations of mental disorders and associated information such as prevalence.
- Does not discuss causation (etiology).
- Offers specific criteria for clinicians to diagnose disorders.
- Takes cultural context, cultural belief systems, and cultural differences between client/worker into account and includes Culture-Bound Syndromes.
- Presents a Defensive Functioning Scale, which assesses the client's defenses or coping patterns at the time of the evaluation and just preceding it.

Definition of intellectual disability in the DSM-5

Intellectual disabilities are neurodevelopmental disorders that include both a cognitive capacity deficit and an adaptive functioning deficit. The onset of an intellectual disability must be during the developmental years. The severity of the disability ranges are mild, moderate, severe, and profound. The severity is determined by the client's adaptive functioning level, rather than the client's cognitive capacity. The DSM-5 has changed the wording of "mental retardation" to intellectual disability to align more closely with other medical, educational, and advocacy groups.

Focus and forms of assessment

Different approaches to social work have different aims for assessment. Assessment may focus on any or all of the following:
- Intrapsychic dynamics, strengths, and problems
- Interpersonal dynamics, strengths, and problems
- Environmental strengths and problems
- The interaction and intersection of intrapsychic, interpersonal, and environmental factors.

The assessment process can take the following form:
- Determine the presenting problem and then determine if there is a match between the problem and available services.
- Ongoing data collection and reassessment.
- Worker will—ask questions, observe behavior/affect, organize data to create a meaningful psychosocial assessment
- Data sources can include—interviews with family members; home visits; contacts with teachers, clergy, doctors, service providers, and friends

Client assessment

Methods
Assessments are ideally multidimensional and use a variety of methods. These may include interviews (both verbal and written), indirect questioning (allusion, sentence completion, etc.), observation, client reports, and collateral contacts (agencies, family, medical providers, schools, etc.). Common assessment approaches include:

- Interviews: using both open-ended questioning (What do you do in your free time?) and closed-ended questioning (How old are you?)
- Social assessment reports (social history): past choices and conduct; basic facts and social data; assessment and data interpretation
- Genograms: a family tree describing relationships in one or more generations
- Ecomaps: a diagram locating a client in a social (including family) environment
- Questionnaires: tools to prompt responses on key issues (depression, etc.)
- Checklists: rapid response tools for summary issues (symptoms, etc.)
- Mental status exams: cognitive evaluations
- Intelligence tests

Process
The first step in client engagement (which often includes cursory exploration of the presenting problem) is to establish rapport. This should be followed by explanations of the treatment process, ethical and legal obligations and limitations to confidentiality, etc. The next step is the completion of a written contract for services. The contract should specify the issues to be addressed, the goals to be pursued, the roles and obligations of each party, and an anticipated course of treatment. Although reasonably explicit, the contract must also be flexible to allow for revision as needed. The process of assessment is typically considered the first stage of treatment. Although assessment begins with the first session, it must continue throughout the course of treatment. During the assessment phase, data and information collection must take place to more fully illuminate the client's problem and any contributing factors. Common domains to be explored include the following: personal (emotional, intellectual, medical, etc.), family, social, community, employment, economic, legal, and spiritual/religious.

Considerations when assessing immigrant client's needs

The following are the areas that a social worker should consider when assessing an immigrant client's needs:

- Why and how did client immigrate?
- What social supports does the client have? (community, relatives)
- Client's education/literacy in language of origin and in English
- Economic and housing resources (including number of people in home, availability of utilities)
- Employment history, ability to find/obtain work
- Client's ability to find and use institutional/governmental supports
- Health status/resources (pre- and post-immigration)
- Social networks (pre- and post-immigration)
- Life control—deree to which he or she experiences personal power and the ability to make choices

Substance related disorders

Substance related disorders and their treatment are discussed below:
- Substance related disorders may be caused by abusing a drug, by medication side-effects, or by exposure to a toxin.
- Substance intoxication or withdrawal includes the behavioral, psychological, and physiological symptoms due to effects of the substance. It will vary depending on type of substance.
- Substance related disorders include the following classes: caffeine; hallucinogens; alcohol, cannabis, stimulants, tobacco, inhalants; opiods, sedatives, hypnotics, and anxiolytics.
- The severity of the particular substance use disorder can be determined by the presence of the number of symptoms, which may include: substance induced delirium, dementia, psychosis, mood disorders, anxiety disorder, sexual dysfunciton, sleep dysfunction.
- Treatment should first focus on the substance. Treatment options include outpatient or inpatient; residential or day care; group, individual, and/or family counseling; methadone maintenance (for opiates); detoxification; self-help groups; or a combination of therapies and medication
- Gambling is now included in substance-related and addictive disorders, as evidence shows that the behaviors of gambling trigger similar reward systems as drugs.

Substance use, abuse, and dependence

Substance abuse alone is considered a less severe condition than substance dependence. Substance abuse is diagnosed when:
1. Major roles and obligations become impaired at home, school and/or work
2. Legal problems ensue (e.g., arrests for driving while intoxicated or disorderly conduct, and/or
3. The abuse continues in spite of related interpersonal and social problems.

Substance dependence refers to the increased use of a substance in order to achieve intoxication, withdrawal symptoms, and continued use in the face of efforts to stop. Medications that are sometimes prescribed to reduce substance use include disulfiram (Antabuse), which causes negative symptoms if alcohol is ingested and naltrexone (ReVia and Trexan), a reward/receptor blocker for alcohol and opiates.

Drug of choice
The following factors may influence an individual's preference for a "drug of choice:"
- Current fashion
- Availability
- Peer influences
- Individual biological and psychological factors
- Genetic factors (especially with alcoholism)

Harm due to method of administration
Harm that may come from the use of illegal drugs due to their method of administration is explained as follows:
- Doses can be unknown, which can lead to drug overdose and death.
- Using contaminated needles can cause staph infections, Hepatitis, or HIV/AIDS.

- Inhalants are frequently toxic and can cause brain damage, heart disease, and kidney or liver failure.

Harm due to behavior

Harm that can result from the behaviors that substance use/abuse can generate is explained as follows:

- Substances that are illegally obtained are often associated with minor crimes, crimes against family members and the community, and prostitution.
- Alcohol is associated with domestic violence, child abuse, sexual misconduct, and serious auto accidents.
- All substances promote behavioral problems that may make it difficult for the individual to obtain/retain employment, or to sustain normal family relationships.

Injuries and illnesses

The following are possible injuries or illnesses that often result from the use of substances:

- Physical damage
- Brain damage
- Organic failure
- Fetal damage when used by pregnant women
- Birth of drug exposed babies who require intensive therapy throughout childhood
- Altering of brain chemistry/permanent brain damage
- Effects on dopamine in brain, which directly affects mood

Related medical problems

Some medical problems that may be directly related to substance use are as follows:

- Cardiac problems (acute cocaine intoxication)
- Respiratory depression and coma (severe opioid overdose and alcohol abuse)
- Hepatic cirrhosis (prolonged heavy drinking)
- Malnutrition (from poor self-care)
- Physical trauma (risk-taking behavior)
- HIV infection (risk-taking behavior)

Conditions associated with those who administer substances by injection:

- Bacterial infections
- HIV
- hepatitis

Predicting factors of substance abuse

Factors contributing to likelihood of substance abuse include the following:

- Early or regular use of "gateway" drugs (alcohol, marijuana, nicotine)
- Intra-familial disturbances.
- Associating with substance-using peers.

Clinical disorders in clients

The following clinical disorders are commonly found in clients with substance use disorders:

- Conduct disorders, particularly the aggressive subtype
- Depression
- Bipolar disorder

- Schizophrenia
- Anxiety disorders
- Eating disorders
- Pathological gambling
- Antisocial personality disorder
- PTSD
- Other personality disorders

Treatment

Substance use disorder treatment includes the following components:
- An assessment phase
- Treatment of intoxication and withdrawal when necessary
- Development of a treatment strategy.

General treatment strategies:
- Total abstinence (drug-free)
- Substitution, or use of alternative medications that inhibit the use of illegal drugs
- Harm reduction

The following psychosocial treatments have been found to be most effective for clients with substance use disorders:
- Cognitive behavioral therapies
- Behavioral therapies
- Psychodynamic/interpersonal therapies
- Group and family therapies
- Participation in self-help groups

Goals of treatment:
- Reducing use and effects of substances
- Abstinence
- Reducing the frequency and severity of relapse
- Improvement in psychological and social functioning

Narcotics

Narcotics are explained as follows:
- Drugs used medicinally to relieve pain.
- They have a high potential for abuse.
- They cause relaxation with an immediate rush.
- Possible effects are restlessness, nausea, euphoria, drowsiness, respiratory depression, constricted pupils.

Indications of misuse

The following are some indications of possible misuse of narcotics:
- Scars (tracks) caused by injections
- Constricted pupils
- Loss of appetite
- Sniffles

- Watery eyes
- Cough
- Nausea
- Lethargy
- Drowsiness
- Nodding
- Syringes, bent spoons, needles, etc.
- Weight loss or anorexia

Overdose symptoms

The symptoms of overdose of narcotics are:
- Slow, shallow breathing
- Clammy skin
- Convulsions
- Coma
- Possible death

Withdrawal

Withdrawal syndrome for narcotics includes the following:
- Watery eyes
- Runny nose
- Yawning
- Cramps
- Loss of appetite
- Irritability
- Nausea
- Tremors
- Panic
- Chills
- Sweating

Depressants

Depressants are explained as follows:
- Drugs used medicinally to relieve anxiety, irritability, or tension.
- They have a high potential for abuse and development of tolerance.
- They produce a state of intoxication similar to that of alcohol.
- When combined with alcohol, their effects increase and their risks are multiplied.

Effects

Possible effects are as follows:
- Sensory alteration, reduction in anxiety, intoxication
- In small amounts, can cause relaxed muscles and calmness
- In larger amounts—slurred speech, impaired judgment, loss of motor coordination
- In very large doses—respiratory depression, coma, death
- Newborn babies of abusers may exhibit dependence, withdrawal symptoms, behavioral problems, and birth defects.

<u>Indications of misuse</u>
Indications of possible misuse include:
- Behavior similar to alcohol intoxication (without the odor of alcohol)
- Staggering, stumbling, lack of coordination
- Slurred speech
- Falling asleep while at work
- Difficulty concentrating
- Dilated pupils

<u>Symptoms of overdose</u>
Symptoms of overdose include:
- Shallow respiration
- Clammy skin
- Dilated pupils
- Weak and rapid pulse
- Coma or death

<u>Withdrawal</u>
Withdrawal syndrome for these substances includes the following:
- Anxiety
- Insomnia
- Muscle tremors
- Loss of appetite
- Abrupt cessation or a greatly reduced dosage may cause convulsions, delirium, or death

Stimulants

Stimulants are drugs used to increase alertness, relieve fatigue, feel stronger and more decisive, for euphoric effects, to counteract the "down" feeling of depressants or alcohol.

<u>Effects</u>
Possible effects include:
- Increased heart rate
- Increased respiratory rate
- Elevated blood pressure
- Dilated pupils
- Decreased appetite

With high doses possible effects include:
- Rapid or irregular heartbeat
- Loss of coordination
- Collapse
- Perspiration
- Blurred vision
- Dizziness
- Feelings of restlessness, anxiety, delusions

Indications of possible misuse include:

- Excessive activity, talkativeness, irritability, argumentativeness, nervousness.
- Increased blood pressure or pulse rate, dilated pupils
- Long periods without sleeping or eating
- Euphoria

Overdose symptoms
Symptoms of overdose include:

- Agitated behavior
- Increase in body temperature
- Hallucinations
- Convulsions
- Possible death

Withdrawal
Withdrawal syndrome for stimulants includes the following:

- Apathy
- Long periods of sleep
- Irritability
- Depression
- Disorientation

Hallucinogens

Hallucinogens are explained as follows:

- Drugs that cause behavioral changes that are often multiple and dramatic.
- No known medical use, but some block sensation to pain and their use may result in self-inflicted injuries.
- "Designer drugs," which are made to imitate certain illegal drugs, can be many times stronger than the drugs they imitate.

The possible effects of hallucinogens include:

- Rapidly changing mood/feelings, immediately and long after use.
- Hallucinations, illusions, dizziness, confusion, suspicion, anxiety, loss of control.
- Chronic use—depression, violent behavior, anxiety, distorted perception of time.
- Large doses—convulsions, coma, heart/lung failure, ruptured blood vessels in the brain.
- Delayed effects—"flashbacks" occurring long after use.
- Designer drugs—possible irreversible brain damage.

Indications of misuse
Indications of possible misuse include:

- Extreme changes in behavior and mood
- Sitting/reclining in a trance-like state
- Individual may appear fearful
- Chills, irregular breathing, sweating, trembling hands
- Changes in sensitivity to light, hearing, touch, smell, and time
- Increased blood pressure, heart rate, blood sugar

<u>Overdose</u>
Symptoms of overdose include:
- Longer, more intense episodes
- Psychosis
- Coma
- Death

Cannabis

Cannabis is the hemp plant from which marijuana (a tobacco like substance) and hashish (resinous secretions of the cannabis plant) are produced.

<u>Effects</u>
Effects of cannabis include:
- Euphoria followed by relaxation
- Impaired memory, concentration, and knowledge retention
- Loss of coordination
- Increased sense of taste, sight, smell, hearing
- Irritation to lungs and respiratory system
- Cancer
- With stronger doses: fluctuating emotions, fragmentary thoughts, disoriented behavior

<u>Indications of misuse</u>
Indications of possible misuse include:
- Animated behavior and loud talking, followed by sleepiness.
- Dilated pupils
- Bloodshot eyes
- Distortions in perception
- Hallucinations
- Distortions in depth and time perception
- Loss of coordination

<u>Overdose symptoms</u>
Symptoms of overdose include:
- Fatigue
- Lack of coordination
- Paranoia

<u>Withdrawal syndrome</u>
The withdrawal symptoms for cannabis include:
- Insomnia
- Hyperactivity
- Sometimes decreased appetite

Alcohol

Alcohol is:
- A liquid distilled product of fermented fruits, grains, and vegetables.
- Can be used as a solvent, an antiseptic, and a sedative.
- Has a high potential for abuse.
- Small to moderate amounts taken over extended periods of time have no negative effects and may have positive health results.

Effects
Its effects include:
- Intoxication
- Sensory alteration
- Reduction in anxiety

Indications of misuse
Indications of possible misuse include:
- Confusion
- Disorientation
- Loss of motor control
- Convulsions
- Shock
- Shallow respiration
- Involuntary defecation
- Drowsiness
- Respiratory depression
- Possible death

Overdose symptoms
Symptoms of overdose include:
- Staggering
- Odor of alcohol on breath
- Loss of coordination
- Dilated pupils
- Slurred speech
- Coma
- Respiratory failure
- Nerve damage
- Liver damage
- Fetal alcohol syndrome (in babies born to alcohol abusers)

<u>Withdrawal syndrome</u>
Symptoms of withdrawal from alcohol include:
- Sweating
- Tremors
- Altered perception
- Psychosis
- Fear
- Auditory hallucinations

<u>Challenges of diagnosing and treating abuse</u>
Particular challenges of alcohol abuse in the context of diagnosis and treatment are explained below:
- Alcohol is the most available and widely used substance.
- Progression of alcoholism dependence often occurs over an extended period of time, unlike some other substances whose progression can be quite rapid. Because of this slow progression, individuals can deny their dependence and hide it from employers for long periods.
- Most alcohol dependent individuals have gainful employment, live with families, and are given little attention until their dependence crosses a threshold, at which time the individual fails in their familial, social, or employment roles.
- Misuse of alcohol represents a difficult diagnostic problem as it is a legal substance. Clients, their families, and even clinicians can claim that the client's alcohol use is normative.
- After friends, family members, or employers tire of maintaining the fiction that the individual's alcohol use is normative, the alcoholic will be more motivated to begin the process of accepting treatment.

Steroids

Steroids are synthetic compounds closely related to the male sex hormone, testosterone, and are available both legally and illegally. They have a moderate potential for abuse, particularly among young males.

<u>Effects</u>
Effects include:
- Increase in body weight
- Increase in muscle mass and strength
- Improved athletic performance
- Improved physical endurance.

<u>Indications of misuse</u>
Indications of possible misuse include:
- Rapid gains in weight and muscle
- Extremely aggressive behavior
- Severe skin rashes
- Impotence, reduced sexual drive
- In female users, development of irreversible masculine traits

<u>Overdose symptoms</u>
Symptoms of overdose include:
- Increased aggressiveness
- Increased combativeness
- Jaundice
- Purple or red spots on body
- Unexplained darkness of skin
- Unpleasant and persistent breath odor
- Swelling of feet, lower legs

<u>Withdrawal syndrome</u>
Withdrawal syndrome may include the following:
- Considerable weight loss
- Depression
- Behavioral changes
- Trembling

ASD

Autism Spectrum Disorder (ASD) has two components in its diagnosis:
- Delays or abnormal functioning in social interaction/language for social communication.
- Restricted repetitive behaviors, interests and activities.

Both of these pieces will be present in the ASD diagnosis.
Severity levels are:
- Level 1—requires support
- Level 2—requires substantial support
- Level 3—requires very substantial support

In the DSM-5, ASD now encompasses four disorders that were previously separate under the DSM-IV: autistic disorder, Asperger's disorder, childhood integrative disorder, and pervasive developmental disorder.

Persons with ASD associated with other known conditions or environmental factors should have the diagnosis written Autism Spectrum Disorder associated with _____ (name of condition, such as Rett Syndrome).

AD/HD

AD/HD is characterized by two symptom domains: inattentiveness and or/hyperactivity and impulsivity. Diagnosis requires symptoms persisting for at least six months as well as symptoms not motivated by anger or wish to displease/spite others. Inattentiveness symptoms (6 required for child diagnosis) include:
- Forgetful in everyday activity
- Easily distracted
- Makes careless mistakes and doesn't give attention to detail
- Difficulty focusing attention
- Does not appear to listen, even when directly spoken to
- Starts tasks but does not follow through

- Frequently loses essential items
- Finds organizing difficult
- Avoids activities that require prolonged mental exertion

Impulsivity/Hyperactivity symptoms (6 required for child diagnosis) include:
- Frequently gets out of chair
- Runs/climbs at inappropriate times
- Frequently talks more than peers
- Often moves hands and feet, or shifts position in seat
- Frequently interrupts others
- Frequently has difficulty waiting on turn
- Frequently unable to enjoy leisure activities silently
- Frequently "on the go" and seen by others as restless
- Often finishes others' sentences before they can

Eating disorders

Pica, rumination disorder, and avoidant/restrictive food intake disorder
Pica is the persistent eating of non-food substances such as paint, hair, sand, cloth, pebbles, etc. Those with pica do not show an aversion to food. Rumination disorder is regurgitation and re-chewing of food. Avoidant/restrictive food intake disorder has four criteria:
- Criteria A—a disruption in eating evidenced by not meeting nutritional needs and failure to gain expected weight or weight loss, nutritional deficiency, requires nutritional supplementation, or interpersonal interference.
- Criteria B—this disruption is not due to lack of food or culture.
- Criteria C –there does not appear to be a problem with the client's body perception.
- Criteria D—the disturbance can't be explained by another medical condition.

Anorexia nervosa
The criteria for anorexia nervosa are as follows:
- Criteria A: extreme restriction of food, lower than requirements, leading to low body weight.
- Criteria B: an irrational fear of gaining weight or behaviors that prevent weight gain, through at low weight
- Criteria C: distorted body image or a lack of acknowledgement of gravity of current weight

Treatment
Treatment for eating disorders includes the following:
- Psychopharmacology
- Individual therapy
- Family therapy
- Medical supervision to monitor weight, vital signs, and blood values
- Hospitalization when necessary for close behavioral and medical supervision

Motor and tic disorders

Motor disorders are a type of neurodevelopmental disorder. Motor disorders can be classified as developmental coordination disorders, stereotypic movement disorders, and tic disorders. Tic disorders are further classified as Tourette's disorder, persistent motor or vocal tic disorder, and provisional tic disorder. Tic disorders are characterized by rapid, recurrent, stereotyped motor movements or vocalizations. Those with Tourette's disorder typically have multiple motor tics and one or more vocal tics. Those with chronic motor or vocal tic disorder have either motor or vocal tics.

Bipolar disorders

The following is a brief overview of the four types of bipolar disorders:
- Bipolar I: at least one manic episode, with or without depressive symptoms
- Bipolar II: hypomanic episodes with at least one major depressive episode in the past
- Cyclothymic disorder: both depressive and hypomanic symptoms falling short of outright mania and major depression
- Bipolar Disorder, NOS (not otherwise specified): sometimes called "sub-threshold bipolar disorder," where cycling mood is evident but difficult to categorize.

A diagnosis is posted by name, primary pole, variation, and severity (e.g., Bipolar I Disorder, Manic Episode, Mixed, Moderate).

The criteria for bipolar I disorder are as follows:
- Criteria A: The client must meet the criteria listed below for at least one manic episode. The manic episode is usually either preceded or followed by an episode of major depression or hypomania.
- Criteria B: The episode cannot be explained by schizophrenia spectrum or other psychotic disorders criteria.

Criteria for a manic episode include:
- Criteria A: An episode of significantly elevated, demonstrative, or irritable mood. There are significant goal-directed behaviors, activities, and an increase in the amount of energy the client normally has. Symptoms are present for most of the day and last at least one week.
- Criteria B: During this period, the client will experience 3 of the following symptoms (if the client presents with only an irritable mood 4 of the following need to be present for diagnosis):
  - Less need for sleep
  - Excessive talking
  - Inflated self-esteem
  - Easily distracted
  - Flight of ideas
  - Engages in activities that have negative consequences
  - Engages in either goal directed activity or purposeless activity
- Criteria C: The episode causes significant impairment socially
- Criteria D: The symptoms cannot be attributed to a substance

Schizophrenia spectrum and other psychotic disorders

The schizophrenia spectrum and other psychotic disorders classification includes:
- Delusional disorder
- Brief psychotic disorder
- Schizophreniform disorder
- Schizophrenia

- Schizoaffective disorder
- Substance/medication-induced psychotic disorder
- Psychotic disorder due to another medical condition
- Catatonia

Schizophrenia criteria for diagnosis include the following:
- Criteria A (client must have at least 2 of the following symptoms):
  o Hallucinations (core positive symptom)*
  o Delusions (core positive symptom)*
  o Disorganized speech (core positive symptom)*
  o Severely disorganized or catatonic behavior
  o Negative symptoms (e.g., avolition, diminished expression)
  *Diagnosis requires at least one of the three core positive symptoms.
- Criteria B: Client's level of functioning is significantly below level prior to onset.
- Criteria C: If the client has not had successful treatment there are continual signs of schizophrenia for more than six months.
- Criteria D: Depressive disorder, bipolar disorder, and schizoaffective disorder have been ruled out.
- Criteria E: The symptoms cannot be attributed to another medical condition or a substance.
- Criteria F: If the client has had a communication disorder or Autism since childhood, a diagnosis of schizophrenia is only made if the client has hallucinations or delusions.

Delusional disorders

These disorders are typified by the presence of a persistent delusion. The delusion may be of the following types: persecutory, jealousy, erotomanic (that someone is in love with the delusional person), somatic (that one has a physical defect or disease), grandiose, or mixed. Criteria for diagnosis are as follows:
- Criteria A: The client experiences at least one delusion for at least one month or longer.
- Criteria B: The client does not meet criteria for schizophrenia.
- Criteria C: Functioning is not significantly impaired, and behavior except dealing specifically with delusion is not bizarre.
- Criteria D: Any manic or depressive episodes are brief.
- Criteria E: The symptoms cannot be attributed to another medical condition or a substance.

It should be specified if the delusions are bizarre. Severity is rated by the quantitative assessment measure "Clinician-Rated Dimensions of Psychosis Symptom Severity."

Mood disorder

Mood disorders are characterized by persistent abnormal mood. This abnormal mood may be either depressed or euphoric. Symptoms of mood disorders may be somatic, affective cognitive, and/or behavioral. Mood disorers cause psychological distress and impaired role functioning.

Treatment
Treatment for mood disorders consists of the following:
- Pharmaceuticals:
  o Antidepressants for major depressive disorder and dysthymia
  o Anti-psychotics if accompanied by psychotic features.

- o Mood stabilizers if bipolar I, bipolar II, or cyclothymia.
- o Consistent administration and monitoring for effectiveness and side effects required.
- Interpersonal/psychodynamic therapy
- Behavioral therapy
- Cognitive therapy
- Group psychotherapy
- Self-help groups

Major depressive disorder

The criteria for major depressive disorder are as follows:
- Criteria A: client experiences 5 or more of the following symptoms during 2 consecutive weeks. These symptoms are associated with a change in the client's normal functioning.
  - o Depressed mood
  - o Loss of ability to feel pleasure or have interest in normal activities
  - o Decreased aptitude for thinking
  - o Thoughts of death
  - o Fatigue (daily)
  - o Inappropriate guilt/worthlessness
  - o Observable motor agitation or psychomotor retardation
  - o Weight change of more or less than 5% in one month
  - o Hypersomnia or insomnia (almost daily)

  (Of the presenting symptoms, either depressed mood or loss of ability to feel pleasure must be included to make this diagnosis.)
- Criteria B: The episode causes distress or social/functional impairment
- Criteria C: The symptoms cannot be attributed to a substance or another condition/disease
- Criteria D: The episode does not meet the criteria for schizophrenia spectrum or other psychotic disorder
- Criteria E: Client does not meet criteria for manic/hypomanic episode

Anxiety disorders

The following are types of anxiety disorders:
- Panic disorder—recurrent brief but intense fear in the form of panic attacks with physiological or psychological symptoms
- Specific phobia—fear of specific situations or objects
- Generalized anxiety disorder—chronic psychological and cognitive symptoms of distress, excessive worry lasting at least 6 mooonths of duration
- Separation anxiety disorder—excessive anxiety related to being separated from someone the client is attached to
- Selective mutism—inability to speak in social settings (when it would seem appropriate) though normally able to speak
- Social anxiety disorder—anxiety about social situations
- Agoraphobia—anxiety about being outside of the home or in open places

The treatment of anxiety disorders consists of the following:
- Short-acting anti-anxiety medications for episodic symptoms (panic attacks) and antidepressants for longer term use (ex. for OCD, social phobia)
- Psychotherapy such as supportive therapy, cognitive behavioral therapy (systematic desensitization), DBT (Dialectical Behavioral Therapy), EMDR for PTSD
- Group therapy
- Inpatient hospitalization (when a threat to self or others)

Somatoform disorders

All somatoform disorders are marked by multiple physical/somatic symptoms that cannot be explained medically. Symptoms impair social or work functioning and cause distress.
- Somatic symptom disorder—somatic symptoms (including pain) that are persistent and distressing about which feelings regarding these symptoms take up an extremely large amount of time and energy.
- Illness anxiety disorder—preoccupation with getting or currently having an illness
- Factitious disorder—falsely presenting oneself or someone else as ill, even when there are no obvious gains in doing so
- Conversion disorder (functional neurological symptom disorder)—motor or perceptual symptoms suggesting physical disorder, but actually reflect emotional conflicts
- Psychological factors affecting other medical conditions—the client has a medical condition that is adversely affected by psychological behavior

Treatment
The treatment of somatoform disorders consists of the following:
- No definitive treatment. Goal is early diagnosis in order to circumvent unnecessary medical/surgical intervention.
- Attempt to move attention from symptoms to problems of living.
- Supportive therapy to help the individual cope with symptoms.
- Long-term relationship with single physician.
- No medication.

Dissociative disorders

These are all characterized by a disturbance in the normally integrative functions of identity, memory, consciousness, or environmental perception:
- Dissociative identity disorder (previously multiple personality disorder)—two or more personalities exist within one person, with each personality dominant at a particular time.
- Dissociative amnesia—inability to recall important personal data, more than forgetfulness. Is not due to organic causes and comes on suddenly.
- Depersonalization/derealization disorder—feeling detached from one's mental processes or body, as if one is an observer.

Treatment is primarily done via psychotherapy, with the goals of working through unconscious conflict or recovering traumatic memories, and integrating feeling states with memories or events.

Personality disorders

Criteria
The following are the criteria for personality disorders:
- Criteria A: long-term pattern of maladaptive personality traits and behaviors that do not align with the client's culture. These traits and behaviors will be found in at least two of the following areas
  - Impulse control
  - Inappropriate emotional intensity or responses
  - Inappropriately interpreting people, events, and self
  - Inappropriate social functioning
- Criteria B: The traits and behaviors are inflexible and exist despite changing social situations
- Criteria C: The traits and behaviors cause distress and impair functioning
- Criteria D: Onset was adolescence or early adulthood and has been enduring
- Criteria E: The behaviors and traits are not due to another mental disorder
- Criteria F: The behaviors and traits are not due to a substance

Treatment
The treatment of personality disorders is as follows:
- Purpose of intervention is to alleviate symptoms, decrease social/emotional disability, or deal with interpersonal/societal need for symptom management
- Psychotherapy is used to promote recognition of the client's covert dependence and unexpressed fearfulness.
- Worker should place importance on awareness of counter-transference issues because of treatment-resistant behaviors, including mistrust of the worker, lack of boundaries, and lack of recognition of the worker as a person

Psychopharmacology is not generally used.

OCD and PTSD

Obsessive-compulsive disorder is diagnosed when obsessions (intrusive thoughts) and compulsions (behavioral urges) dominate an individual's life to the extent that academic, occupational, or social functioning is disrupted. Posttraumatic stress disorder refers to a constellation of symptoms following an event which threatens life, serious injury, or emotional integrity. Symptoms include recurrent intrusive recollections, dreams, anger, distraction, irritability, sleep disturbance, hypervigilance and/or an exaggerated startle response. Common treatment medications include those for anxiety and depression.

Psychiatric disorders common during childhood and adolescence

The following are six psychiatric disorders common in childhood and adolescence:
- Attention Deficit/Hyperactivity Disorder (AD/HD): persistent hyperactivity/impulsivity and/or inattention in two or more key situations (home, school, work) with symptoms present prior to 7 years of age
- Autism Spectrum Disorder (ASD): deficits in communication and social interaction, often including persistent repetitive behaviors such as head banging and/or rocking, with symptoms present before 3 years of age

- 38 -

- Conduct Disorder: persistent violations of standards of proper behavior, including aggression toward people and animals, deceit, destruction of property, running away, theft, truancy, etc., in someone under the age of 18 (when 18+ the behavior is diagnosed as antisocial personality disorder)
- Encopresis: persistent defecation in inappropriate places when over the age of 4
- Enuresis: persistent urination (whether voluntary or involuntary) when over the age of 5
- Separation Disorder: exaggerated distress at separation from figures of attachment when under the age of 18

ODD

Oppositional Defiant Disorder (ODD) refers to an ongoing pattern of disobedient, defiant, and hostile behavior (e.g., argumentativeness, blaming, spitefulness, vindictiveness) toward those in authority sufficient to compromise function in social, academic, or occupational settings. The symptoms cannot be the result of another disorder, such as the more serious conduct disorder, depression anxiety, psychosis, etc., with persistent evidence for at least six months.

Warning signs and risk of suicide

The warning signs of suicide include the following:
- Depression
- Prior suicide attempts
- Family suicide history
- Abrupt increase in substance abuse
- Reckless and impulsive behavior
- Isolation
- Poor coping
- Support system loss
- Recent or anticipated loss of someone special
- Verbal expression of feeling out of control
- Preoccupation with death
- Behavioral changes not otherwise explained

Where risk of suicide is suspected, the client should be questioned directly about any thoughts of self-harm. This should be followed by a full assessment and history (particularly family history of suicide). Where the threat of suicide is not imminent and the client is amenable to intervention, a written "no-suicide contract" may be considered; the client will agree in the contract to contact the suicide hotline, the social worker, or some other specified professional. Where a client already has a plan, or has multiple risk factors, hospitalization must be arranged. If any immediate attempt has already been made, a medical evaluation must occur immediately.

Abuse evaluation

Social workers are mandated reporters and must report all suspected cases of child abuse, in addition to "dependent adult" and elder abuse. When assessing for signs of physical abuse, note particularly the following:
- Bruises, burns, cuts, or welts, and note if they are in various stages of healing;
- Attempts by the victim to hide injuries;
- Exaggerated efforts to please parents/caregivers;

- Major behavioral problems or disturbances (violence, withdrawal, self-injury, etc.)
- Hypervigilance around adults, especially parents/caregivers

Signs of psychological or emotional abuse include the following:
- Depression
- Withdrawal
- Preoccupation with details;
- Repetitive, agitated, and/or rhythmic movements
- Evidence of unreasonable demands or conflict triangulation (e.g., drawing a child into marital conflicts)

Signs of neglect include the following:
- Inappropriate dress
- Poor hygiene
- Failure-to-thrive symptoms (retarded development, underweight, hair loss, begging for food, etc.)
- Poor supervision;
- Significant fatigue
- Missed school and/or medical appointments
- Untreated health problems
- Inadequate sleeping situation

Follow up after identifying child, dependent adult, or elder adult abuse

After abuse has been determined, a full report must be made to the appropriate agency, initially by telephone with a written report to follow. For social workers employed by such agencies, a follow-up plan of action must be determined. The level of risk must be evaluated, including the perpetrator's relationship to the victim, prior history of abusive behavior, and severity of harm inflicted, as well as the victim's age, health situation, cognitive capacity and psychological status, available support systems, and capacity for self-protection given that the abuse is now in the open. Follow-up options include:
- Reports for criminal prosecution
- Home visits
- Removal from the home
- Alternative caregiver/guardian appointments through courts, etc.

Safety is the primary concern and is above all else.

Sexual abuse

Some of the more common signs of sexual abuse are:
1. Genital injuries (abrasions, bruises, scars, tears, etc.)
2. Blood in the underwear (e.g., from vaginal and/or rectal injuries)
3. Complaints of genital discomfort and/or excessive grabbing of the genital area
4. Any diagnosis of a sexually transmitted disease
5. Frequent urinary tract and bladder infections
6. Complaints of stomachache when coupled with other signs
7. Abrasions or bruises to the thighs and legs
8. Enuresis (bed-wetting) and/or encopresis (fecal soiling)

9. Behavioral disturbances (acting out, self-destructive behavior, overly precocious and/or aggressive sexual behavior, promiscuity, etc.
10. Depression
11. Eating disorders
12. Fears and phobias
13. Dissociation
14. Any unexplained or sudden appearance of money, toys, or gifts

Direct and Indirect Practice

Mandated reporting of abuse

Social work is one of several professions that are under so-called legal "mandate" to report cases of abuse. It is not necessary to have witnessed the abuse, nor must one have incontrovertible evidence. Rather, there need only be sufficient cause to "suspect" in order for a report to be required. If the report is made "in good faith," the reporting party is immune from liability—both from reporting (should the allegations prove unfounded) and from the liability that would otherwise accrue from any failure to report actual abuse. Abuse may be physical, emotional, sexual, or constitute neglect. All states mandate the reporting of child abuse, and most mandate the reporting of "dependent adult" abuse (adults who are developmentally delayed and thus mentally infirm or elderly persons unable to protect themselves due to either physical or mental frailty). Where dependent abuse reporting is not mandated, complex situations may occur. Know your state's laws and seek advice when necessary.

Mainstreaming/normalization and juvenile status offense

Mainstreaming or normalization is including children with special needs in regular classrooms, while continuing to give them special services. A juvenile status offense is a crime that has no equivalent in the adult criminal code that can only be committed by children. Examples include truancy, running away, etc.

Active threat of homicidality

A client may be deemed a threat to others if
1. He or she makes a serious threat of physical violence, and
2. The threat is made against a specifically named individual(s).

If the threat is also made in the context of a clinician–patient relationship, then a "duty to protect" is also generated. In such a situation, a clinician is duty bound not only to notify appropriate authorities and agencies charged to protect the citizenry, but to also make a good-faith effort to warn the intended victim(s) or, failing that, someone who is reasonably believed able to warn the intended victim(s). The duty to warn stems from the 1976 legal case *Tarasoff v. Regents of the University of California,* where a therapist heard a credible threat and called only law enforcement authorities, failing to notify the intended victim. The murder occurred, and the case was appealed to the California Supreme Court, from which the rubric of duty to protect an intended victim has been established.

Crisis intervention

The social worker should have specific expertise in the crisis area (grief, trauma, etc.), and should present as authoritative and direct in order to enhance client stability and reduce feelings of vulnerability. Care should be taken to prevent over-attachment of the client to the social worker. The nature of a crisis limits the time available for assessment, which must thus be focused on the immediate issues. However, it should include exploration of the events surrounding the crisis, the client's current responses and past response patterns in similar situations, and available support systems and resources. Treatment involves examination of the precipitating events, the thoughts and emotions evoked, the skills needed to cope, and the development of sufficient supports and resources to facilitate crisis resolution. Treatment techniques may vary but tend to involve problem-solving strategies.

Crisis intervention derives its theoretical orientation from ego psychology, psychoanalytic theory, and social learning theory. Key tenets include:
- Interventions are limited to a time of crisis, defined as any highly stressful, disturbing, or disastrous event that leaves an individual unable to cope using existing coping resources.
- A crisis tends to elicit unpredictable behaviors and responses, leaving the individual uniquely malleable to intervention and change.
- A series of predictable stages ensues (a.k.a. the "crisis sequence"): (a) the crisis event, (b) feelings of anxiety and vulnerability when coping skills are overwhelmed, (c) the "last straw" factor or event that causes a search for help, (d) emotional turmoil and disequilibrium, and (e) engagement of new coping skills, leading to crisis resolution.
- Individuals in crisis may not be "dysfunctional" (e.g., need no DSM diagnosis).
- The goal is to enhance coping capacity (not affect a "cure"); other life issues are dealt with only if related to the current crisis.
- Crisis intervention is short term and terminates when the immediate crisis is resolved.

Ways in which change occurs

One can view the way that change occurs within the client in different ways. The different approaches to social work may frame the same changes in different language. Below are three examples:
1. Psychological (e.g., psychodynamic, behavioral, cognitive, etc.)
2. Sphere of change (e.g., individual, couple, family, social system, etc.)
3. Goal of change (e.g., personality, behavioral, social system, etc.)

Practice frameworks

Social work "practice frameworks" serve as a frame of reference and basis from which to address client issues or problems. The criteria for selection of a practice framework include:
1. The kind of problem presenting
2. The relevant psychological theoretical orientation
3. The form of treatment needed/available (e.g., individual, family, group)
4. The outcomes/goals sought, and
5. The available time and resources

The application of additional practice frameworks may be necessary over the course of the treatment process. Thus, the social worker should develop facility in multiple frameworks in order to facilitate client treatment and to meet the goals and needs of the agency or institution in which the social worker is employed.

Five common practice frameworks used by social workers with their clients are explained below:
1. The generalist framework is a broad, eclectic, flexible approach that is open to the application of multiple theories, models, and methods of intervention. At the opposite end of this continuum is the specialist approach, which would be limited to a single theoretical orientation and intervention approach.

2. The systems framework engages the biological and social aspects of human behavior and focuses on the interface between the client's behavior and the social environment in relation to the presenting issue or problem. The ecosystems framework evaluates client behaviors from the perspective of environmental adaptation.
3. The culturally-sensitive framework places a client's culture, ethnicity, and religious perspectives central to the assessment and intervention process.
4. The feminist framework is applied when issues of gender, roles, stereotyping, and discrimination are of primary concern.
5. The strengths framework examines and capitalizes on a client's strengths to achieve the necessary outcomes.

Major approaches to social work practice

The major approaches to social work practice are:
- Psychosocial
- Functional
- Problem-solving
- Behavior modification
- Cognitive therapy
- Crisis intervention
- Task centered and competency-based treatment
- Life model (ecological treatment)
- Family therapy
- Narrative therapy
- Play therapy
- Geriatric social work
- Trauma treatment

Psychoanalytic approach

The psychoanalytic (or psychodynamic) intervention approach draws upon psychoanalytic theory, ego psychology theory, psychosocial theory, and object relations theory. Key tenets of this intervention approach include:
1. The social environment is the primary external influence.
2. Behavior is seen as emerging from unconscious motives and drives.
3. Dysfunction is rooted in stress-producing experiences and conflicts in the unconscious mind.
4. Problem resolution is brought about by drawing repressed information into the conscious mind and using the energy from the stress of this process to overcome conflict and induce change.

Key barriers to this process are the defense mechanisms, as well as transference (the client's unconscious issues, feelings, desires, and defenses involving the worker) and countertransference (the worker's unconscious issues, feelings, desires, and defenses involving the client). The role of the social worker is focused on resolving conflict.

From a psychoanalytic intervention approach, assessment is a continuous process throughout treatment. Key elements of assessment include:
1. identifying and overcoming defense mechanisms that are barriers to progress

2. identifying and understanding the etiology of various conflicts impeding the change process (the how and why of the conflicts discovered)
3. Observation of body language, verbal expressions, narration, and word selection in descriptions of life experiences to better identify unconscious motivations, drives, and other influences impacting the issue(s) of concern.

The psychoanalytic approach uses numerous techniques in the treatment process, including
1. Free association (encouraging a client to relate anything that comes to mind in order to examine unconscious thinking, distortions, hidden desires, etc.)
2. Confrontation (the bringing together of opposing ideas for purposes of exploration) to overcome "resistance" (client avoidance of difficult memories and experiences, resulting in delayed growth and progress)
3. "Delving" (exploring the client's past for clues to current circumstances, thinking, desires, fears, and motivations)
4. Dream analysis (analyzing and interpreting dreams in search of unconscious desires, fears, and motivations)
5. Ventilation (releasing difficult thoughts and emotions)
6. Sustainment (accepting, encouraging, reassuring to bolster client confidence);
7. Direct influence (advising and encouraging specific behaviors and changes to achieve desired goals).

The phases of treatment include
1. Engagement (building trust and rapport)
2. Contracting (identifying goals, boundaries, and the course of treatment)
3. Ongoing treatment (issue resolution in a manner to optimize current functioning)
4. Termination (reviewing and summarizing progress and planning future independent steps for progress maintenance and continued growth).

Behavioral approach

The behavioral (or behavioral modification) intervention approach draws upon behavioral theory, classical (respondent) conditioning theory, operant conditioning theory, and social learning theory. Key tenets of this intervention approach include:
1. The focus is on observable behavior as opposed to underlying emotions and mental disorders.
2. Behavioral evaluation replaces exploration of the past or of the unconscious mind.
3. Conscious choices to change are sufficient to overcome dysfunctional behaviors.
4. Behavioral modification techniques can induce both conscious/voluntary change, and behavioral conditioning and reinforcement (i.e., combining dysfunctional behavior with a negative effect) can induce unconscious change.
5. Change occurs only when behaviors are specifically identified, operationally defined, and coupled with consequences that can be controlled.
6. Change is most rapid and enduring when the client voluntarily desires to change.

In this framework the role of the social worker is less significant in terms of the therapist-client relationship than that involved in a psychoanalytic approach. Even so, it should be supportive, understanding, and facilitative in order to sustain the difficult process of change.

Treatment techniques in a behavioral approach largely involve the identification of the antecedents and consequences of dysfunctional behaviors in need of change, and the establishment of new antecedents and consequences to facilitate and maintain desirable changes. In this process, however, the social worker may also assign the client to maintain a "behavioral journal." In this journal, the client will make detailed notes about when dysfunctional behaviors occur, any evident triggers for the behavior, the feeling during and after the behavior, etc. In this way the frequency, intensity, and patterns associated with target behaviors can be identified and monitored. Reinforcement and conditioning techniques will then be implemented and refined to better reinforce desirable behaviors and extinguish dysfunctional behaviors.

The phases of treatment involve:
1. Identifying dysfunctional behaviors
2. Prioritizing behaviors in need of change
3. Operationally defining the behaviors (identifying related antecedents and necessary consequences
4. Putting change interventions into motion
5. Monitoring for behavioral change for goal achievement, and
6. Identifying new antecedents and consequences for the next prioritized behavior targeted for change.

Treatment contracting involves creating a formal agreement between the social worker and the client that specifically:
- Identifies the "target behavior"
- Sets new behavioral antecedents and consequences (that are wholesome and functional)
- Specifies the response to contract violations
- Specifies necessary positive reinforcers used to maintain desired behavioral change
- Specifies necessary negative reinforcers to be used if dysfunctional behaviors reemerge, and
- Identifies the indices and methods of monitoring (tallies, charts, etc.) to evaluate the intervention process. The contract must be revised, renewed, and updated as necessary.

Cognitive approach

In the cognitive approach, the role of the social worker is educational, facilitative, and collaborative in pursuing and achieving the client's goals. The process of client assessment is focused on identifying and clarifying the client's specific false beliefs, distortions, and misconceptions as related to the area of concern. The phases of treatment following the assessment phase include in-depth issue clarification, goal setting, contracting between the social worker and client (formalizing agreements regarding the course of treatment, its scope, and overarching goals), education (regarding misconceptions, thought triggers, and resultant behaviors), cognitive reconstruction, progress monitoring, outcome evaluation, and treatment termination. The cognitive approach derives its theoretical orientation from cognitive theory. Key features of this intervention approach include:
1. A problem-focused, goal-oriented approach to the process of personal growth and change
2. A focus on the present as opposed to the past
3. A belief that all emotions and behaviors experienced and exhibited by an individual result from specific thoughts and processes of cognition
4. A belief that behavioral change results when an individual's false beliefs, distortions, and misconceptions are identified, challenged, and revised to produce more functional beliefs, emotions, thoughts, and behaviors, and
5. Incorporation of an educational component by which the client is taught how to identify and revise problematic thinking independently.

Treatment techniques utilized in the cognitive approach include:
1. Clarification: feedback to aid the client to see misperceptions, distortions, and false beliefs more clearly;
2. Explanation: educating the client to better recognize, understand, and correct cognitive errors, along with the identification of triggers and related thought processes and behaviors that must be dealt with for problem resolution to occur;
3. Interpretation: providing extrapolative explanations and theoretical linkages to enhance insight and understanding;
4. Writing assignments: a process by which the client deconstructs misperceptions, distortions, and false beliefs, usually by writing down a description of events and/or thoughts and then examining the narrative for accuracy and rationality;
5. Paradoxical direction: directing the client to pursue the specific behavior targeted for change to increase awareness and enhance the client's sense of control over it; and
6. Reflection: stimulating a client to examine relevant feelings and thoughts to enhance understanding and insight.

Gestalt approach

The role of the social worker in Gestalt therapy is that of a facilitator who aids the individual to become more holistically aware of the self, as it is assumed that the individual already possesses all the necessary tools for change and growth once awareness is expanded and the need for personal responsibility is clear. This requires a positive, supportive, and warm working relationship. Assessment focuses on the level of a client's awareness and insights into personal understanding. The Gestalt approach departs from other therapy approaches in that assessment need not focus on a client's cognitive, emotional, physical, psychological, or social condition, or on a DSM diagnosis. These are superfluous to the change process, which requires only individual awareness and insight into behavioral responsibility. Treatment phases, however, are similar to those seen in other approaches, including the identification of presenting problems/issues, setting goals, and contracting together regarding the goals, course, and scope of treatment.

The Gestalt approach derives its theoretical orientation from Gestalt theory. Key features of this intervention approach include:
1. The premise that every individual has the capacity for growth and change
2. Awareness that the feelings related to any given change can facilitate the change process
3. Treatment that remains client focused (not problem focused)
4. Awareness of the "whole self" (the inner and outer self, one's past experiences, and the lived environment) as being essential to change
5. Taking responsibility for the behaviors we choose to the extent that we become aware of and understand those behaviors, and
6. Awareness that current personal behaviors will lead naturally to the selection of enhanced behaviors as the individual begins to understand and take responsibility for the consequences of those behaviors.

Treatment techniques and concepts utilized in the Gestalt approach include:
- Dialogue (the "empty chair" technique), where the client is directed to communicate with someone with whom conflict exists but who is not actually present
- Enactment of dreams: the acting out of key features of a dream; (3) rehearsal: the process of practicing a certain feeling, thought, or behavior in preparation for change

- Exposing the obvious: bringing certain thoughts, actions, or statements originating with the client to his or her awareness
- Exaggeration: a dramatization of some physical or verbal action in order to enhance awareness.

Key conceptual barriers to change include:
- Confluence: an unrealistic emphasis on similarities to the overreduction or exclusion of differences
- Introjection: the inappropriate acceptance and internalization of messages from others
- Projection: attributing the unacceptable or undesirable aspects of one's own personality to another individual
- Retroflection: doing to oneself what one wishes to do to another.

Task-centered approach

The role of the social worker is primarily facilitative and supportive in assisting the client as requested without interjecting hidden goals or agendas. Assessment focuses on evaluating client-selected behaviors for change, identifying change barriers and associated behaviors, and refining goals and relevant objectives. Phases of treatment involve goal identification, objective clarification (e.g., steps to achieve the goals), the development of a formal contract (with detailed content covering behavioral goals, steps for change, treatment duration, and cost, revised as needed), treatment, and termination. Treatment involves identification of skills and actions for task accomplishment practice by the client (both during and between sessions), progress review, and treatment plan revision. Termination occurs in accordance with the contract and involves progress review and finalizing plans to maintain and further the change process. Direct treatment techniques are typically drawn from behavioral or cognitive-behavioral therapy.

The task-centered approach derives its theoretical orientation from behavioral theory, cognitive theory, and social learning theory. Key features of this intervention approach include:
- The focus is on solely behavioral issues that the client wishes to change, rather than on those that the social worker views as in need of change.
- Behaviors are chosen and perpetuated by the individual, rather than behavior arising from influences of the environment or through learning.
- All behaviors are made consciously and are entirely controlled by the individual, who is capable of changing them.
- The desire to change is central to success (clients treated involuntarily would not fully benefit).
- Change is facilitated when the social worker suggests helpful environmental changes, supports client self-esteem, and clarifies the problem and the objectives needed for its resolution.
- Treatment is short term: 6–12 sessions over a period of several months.

Family therapy approach

The role of the social worker is to educate, facilitate, and serve as a role model. Although actively involved in the therapeutic process, the social worker should remain neutral and direct the family members' attention toward each other in order to observe their patterns of interaction with each other. Assessment is ongoing and primarily involves observations regarding functional and dysfunctional aspects of the family system and subsystems. The phases of treatment include problem identification, goal setting, contracting, and termination. Types of therapies utilized include:

- Family therapy: treating the family as a whole, to improve patterns of interaction and overall functioning
- Collaborative therapy: individual family member treatment by two or more clinicians, coordinating their efforts
- Complementary therapy: a family or group therapy adjunct to individual therapy (e.g., treating a family member for anger issues may involve referring the client to an anger management or family therapy group).

The family therapy approach derives its theoretical orientation from a variety of communication theories and sociological concepts. Key concepts of this intervention approach include:

- The family system is intended to be a source of affection, comfort, nurturing, and security.
- Family dysfunction can impact an individual both personally and socially.
- The family comprises three subsystems: the spousal subsystem, the parent–child subsystem, and the sibling subsystem.
- Each subsystem can affect both of the others, as well as the entire family system, when dysfunction or conflict is present.
- To be effective, treatment should be directed at a presenting problem, rather than attempting to engage all issues that may arise.
- Effective treatment will clarify roles and relationships and improve the quality of intra-familial communication.

Treatment approaches used in family therapy include:

- The communications approach, derived from the concept that poor communication is inherent in family dysfunction and requiring the social worker to prompt family members to listen more carefully and express themselves more plainly, openly, and honestly
- The strategic family therapy approach, which requires the social worker to select and apply strategies to overcome and enhance previously poor family patterns of behavior and dysfunctional family rules
- The structural approach, which calls for structural clarification of the roles, expectations, and responsibilities of all family members
- The social learning approach, which focuses on developing family skills in communication and conflict resolution, while also enhancing patterns of family behavior through behavioral therapy strategies
- The narrative approach, which derives from the concept that dysfunctional thinking and behaviors are rooted in deep-seated ideas, thoughts, and conceptions derived from personal stories (e.g., "narratives") and that change is achieved by the fabrication of new stories or alternate endings to previously handicapping narratives.

Systems theory

Systems theory derives its theoretical orientation from general systems theory and includes elements of organizational theory, family theory, group behavior theory, and a variety of sociological constructs. Key principles include:

- Systems theory endeavors to provide a methodological view of the world by synthesizing key principles from its theoretical roots.
- A fundamental premise is that key sociological aspects of individuals, families, and groups cannot be separated from the whole (i.e., aspects that are systemic in nature).

- All systems are interrelated, and change in one will produce change in the others.
- Systems are either open or closed: open systems accept outside input and accommodate, while closed systems resist outside input due to rigid and impenetrable barriers and boundaries.
- Boundaries are lines of demarcation identifying the outer margins of the system being examined.
- Entropy refers to the process of system dissolution or disorganization.
- Homeostatic balance refers to the propensity of systems to reestablish and maintain stability.

Eco-systems theory

Eco-systems (or "life model") theory derives its theoretical orientation from ecology, systems theory, psychodynamic theory, behavioral theory, and cognitive theory. Key principles include:
- There is an interactive relationship between all living organisms and their environment (both social and physical).
- The process of adaptation is universal and is a reciprocal process by individuals and environments mutually accommodating each other to obtain a "goodness of fit."
- Changes in either individuals or their environments (or both) can be disruptive and produce dysfunction.
- Eco-systems theory works to optimize goodness of fit by modifying perceptions, thoughts, responsiveness, and exchanges between clients and their environments.
- On a larger (community) level, treatment interventions by the eco-systems approach are drawn from direct practice and include educating, identifying and expanding resources, developing needed policies and programs, and engaging governmental systems to support requisite change.

Group therapy approach

The group therapy approach derives its theoretical orientation from a variety of sources, including behavioral theory, cognitive theory, Gestalt theory, and psychoanalytic theory. Individuals may attend groups voluntarily (e.g, as recommended by a social worker) or involuntarily (by court order, etc.). Voluntary participation is typically the most effective. Key concepts of group therapy include:
- Not all issues and individuals are well suited to group processes. Some issues are too personal or complex, and some individuals are too uncomfortable or disruptive.
- Specific benefits typically accrue, such as: (a) sharing with those who are coping with similar issues and experiences, which can be particularly supportive, as participants readily identify with each other; (b) mutual comfort, derived from a sense of shared challenges; and (c) lower levels of stress and intimidation, because of group support influences.
- Group therapy is typically a "complementary therapy" to individual therapy, rather than the sole treatment experience in itself.

The role of the social worker in a group has many facets, including:
- Facilitator for gatekeeping (screening new members), reducing attrition, keeping group dynamics "safe" (preventing subgrouping, scapegoating, etc.), providing supplemental education, etc.;
- Fostering a nurturing and successful learning environment;
- Providing and modeling unconditional positive regard for all members;

- Providing individual support: knowing all members' names, accommodating cultural issues, showing respect, etc.;
- Building group cohesion, modeling inclusiveness via direct eye contact (where culturally appropriate), and showing meaningful attentiveness to all participating;
- Using self-disclosure only where appropriate, only later (after trust exists), and only for the benefit of the group (rather than to meet self-needs) by determining the timing and purpose of any disclosures in advance and with a clear purpose;
- Using body language that is inclusive and open (facing the members, sitting in the circle, arms not crossed over the chest, etc).

Phases of treatment in a group context

The first phase of treatment is the "engagement phase," including
- Gaining members' commitment to attend and participate
- Contracting a clear and complete statement of each member's commitment to participate and the social worker and agency's commitment to remain involved, along with a clearly focused purpose (generally, the more specialized and focused, the greater the group's success).
- Assessment is ongoing, following group processes, dynamics, needs, and goals.

The middle phase includes:
- Refining the group's purpose
- Ensuring successful group mechanics and comfort
- Enhancing purposeful, valued, and productive group interactions.

The ending phase includes:
- Early planning for termination, leaving ample time for all group members to come to grips with closure and separation
- Finalizing group goals and identifying goals that should continue beyond the group's existence.

Advantages

The following are some advantages of group work:
- Members can help others dealing with the same issues and can identify with others in the same situation.
- Sometimes people can more easily accept help from peers than from professionals.
- Through consensual validation, members feel less violated and more reassured as they discover that their problems are similar to those of others.
- Groups give opportunities to members for experimentation and testing new social identities/roles.
- Group practice is not a replacement for individual treatment. Group work is an essential tool for many workers and can be the method of choice for some problems.
- Group practice can complement other practice techniques.

Purposes and goals of group practice

Group practice takes a multiple-goals perspective to solving individual and social problems and is based on the recognition that group experiences have many important functions and can be designed to achieve any or all of the following:
- Providing restorative, remedial, or rehabilitative experiences.
- Helping prevent personal and social distress or breakdown.

- Facilitating normal growth and development, especially during stressful times during the life-cycle.
- Achieving greater degree of self-fulfillment and personal enhancement.
- Helping individuals become active, responsible participants in society through group associations.

Specific group structures
Groups may have varying structures. These include:
- Closed groups: highly controlled groups with criteria for membership, size, location, number of sessions, etc. (e.g., a 10-week grief group), where new members are not allowed, providing a more intimate, cohesive group structure
- Open groups: loosely structured, with members who have made no commitment and may join or leave at any time (e.g., weight-loss groups)
- Short-term groups: between one to a few meetings for a particular event or purpose (pregnancy, parenting, etc.)
- Natural groups: a collection of individuals formed informally (recently divorced friends, etc.) joined later by a social work facilitator
- Formed groups: created purposely and specifically for a common issue or goal (e.g., a court-ordered drunk driving group).

Stages of group development
Groups tend to move through five developmental stages:
1. Preaffiliation: becoming acquainted and deciding whether or not to participate; the group turns to the facilitator for considerable direction
2. Power and control: group member roles form, and natural leaders emerge; challenges for power may occur
3. Intimacy: bonding begins and appreciation and respect grow for the unique problems each member faces
4. Differentiation: greater diversity of opinion emerges, and variations in thoughts and behaviors become evident
5. Separation: termination occurs, goals should be reviewed, and moving forward should be discussed, allowing for feelings of loss.

Key treatment concepts
Key treatment concepts for group work are as follows:
- The group facilitator should elicit participation from everyone in the group and keep some members from dominating.
- Group cohesion benefits group warmth, stability, cooperation, norming (adherence to group rules and standards), communication, and attendance.
- Scapegoating is unfair displacement of criticism and conflict on a vulnerable group member and is not to occur.
- Sociograms, or charts to depict relationships between group members, are used to analyze group processes and to plan improvements.

Proper group formation
The following criteria should guide group formation:
- A balance between homogeneity and heterogeneity is necessary for both variety and cohesion—sharing common goals yet with different life experiences and backgrounds.

- Size should be considered relative to the topic and purpose of the group, ideally between 8 and 12 members (youth groups should be smaller—pre-adolescent groups: 3–4 members; teen groups: 6–10 members; adults 8–12 members), allowing for intimacy, trust, and variety.
- Composition criteria include ensuring that there is more than one individual of any particular race, gender, sexual orientation, etc. Even numbers limit the likelihood of "odd-one-out" pairs developing.
- The group's focus should be specific enough to ensure consistency of purpose, with similar intellectual levels, language, and experiences among the membership to facilitate bonding and group progress.
- Available resources and member capacity (age, health, mobility, etc.) should be considered in determining group location, costs, session numbers, and meeting length.

Group formation process

The following are key elements of the group formation process:
- The worker makes a clear and uncomplicated statement of purpose, of both the members' stakes in coming together and the agency's (and others') stakes in serving them.
- Describing the worker's part in as simple terms as possible.
- Reaching for member reaction to worker's statement of purpose. Identifying how the worker's statement connects to the members' expectations.
- The worker helps members do the work necessary to develop a working consensus about the contract.
- Recognizing goals and motivations, both manifest and latent, stated and unstated.
- Re-contracting as needed.

Heterogeneity vs. homogeneity in group formation

The issues of heterogeneity vs. homogeneity in group formation are summarzed below:
- A group ought to have sufficient homogeneity to provide stability and generate vitality.
- Groups that focus on socialization and developmental issues or on learning new tasks are more likely to be homogeneous.
- Groups that focus on disciplinary issues or deviance are more likely to be heterogeneous.
- Composition and purposes of groups are ultimately influenced or determined by agency goals.

Types of social work groups

The following are the different types of social work groups:
- Educational groups, which focus on helping members learn new information and skills. Educational groups are organized to teach and share skills and information on a specific topic (e.g., single parenting).
- Growth groups, which provide opportunities for members to develop deeper awareness of their own thoughts, feelings, and behavior as well as develop their individual potentialities (e.g., values clarification, consciousness-raising, etc.). Growth groups are organized to enhance individual experience, understanding, and other measures of personal growth and development. Participants need not have any pathology, where overall growth or personal improvement is the goal.
- Remedial groups (or "psychotherapy groups"), which provide support, treatment, and motivation for change in a specific area (e.g., anger management, obsessive-compulsive behavior);

- Self-help groups, which empower individuals to make essential change through the encouragement of others seeking similar progress (e.g., Alcoholics Anonymous)
- Socialization groups, which help members learn social skills and socially accepted behaviors and help members function more effectively in the community. Socialization groups facilitate the enhancement of interpersonal skills, often using games and recreational activities.
- Support groups (or "mutual sharing groups"), which facilitate participant sharing, encouragement, information exchange, etc., among those with common concerns (e.g., widows, single parents)
- Therapy groups, which are designed to help members change their behavior by learning to cope and improve personal problems and to deal with physical, psychological, or social trauma.
- Task groups, which are formed to meet organizational, client, and community needs and functions. Task groups are created to facilitate the achievement of a specific goal (e.g., developmentally delayed adults learning to live independently).

Importance of relationships in group work

The importance of relationships in group work methodology is discussed below:
- Establishing meaningful, effective, relationships is essential and its importance cannot be overemphasized. The worker will form multiple and changing relationships with individual group members, with sub-groups, and with the group as a whole.
- There are multiple other parties who have a stake in members' experiences, such as colleagues of the worker, agency representatives, relatives, friends, and others. The worker will relate differentially to all of these.

Closed groups

Closed groups are described below:
- Convened by workers.
- Members begin the experience together, navigate it together, and end it together at a predetermined time (set number of sessions).
- Closed groups afford better opportunities than open groups for members to identify with each other.
- Give greater stability to the helping situation; stages of group development progress more powerfully.
- Greater amount and intensity of commitment due to same participants being counted on for their presence.

Open groups

Open groups are described below:
- Open groups allow participants to enter and leave according to their choice.
- A continuous group can exist, depending on frequency and rate of membership changes.
- Focus shifts somewhat from the whole group process to individual members' processes.
- With membership shifts, opportunities to use group social forces to help individuals may be reduced. Group will be less cohesive, less available as a therapeutic instrument.
- Worker is kept in a highly central position throughout the life of the group, as he or she provides continuity in an open structure.

Short-term groups

Short-term groups are described below:
- Short term groups are formed around a particular theme or in order to deal with a crisis.
- Limitations of time preclude working through complex needs or adapting to a variety of themes or issues.
- The worker is in the central position in a short term group.

Formed groups

Formed groups are described below:
- Deliberately developed to support mutually agreed-upon purposes.
- Organization of group begins with realization of need for group services.
- Purpose is established by identification of common needs among individuals in an agency or worker caseload.
- Worker guided in interventions and timing by understanding of individual and interpersonal behavior related to purpose.
- It is advisable to have screening, assessment, and preparation of group members.
- Different practice requirements for voluntary and non-voluntary groups as members will respond differently to each.

Stresses experienced during beginning phase of group process

The stress that the worker might experience in beginning phases of a group's process is summarized below:
- Anxiety regarding gaining acceptance by the group.
- Integrating group self-determination with an active leadership role.
- Fear of creating dependency and self-consciousness in group members which would deter spontaneity.
- Difficulty observing and relating to multiple interactions.
- Uncertainty about worker's own role.

Intervention and development stages of group work

The intervention and development stages of the worker in work with groups are summarized below:
- Power and control stage—consists of limit setting, clarification, use of the program
- Intimacy stage—consists of handling transference, rivalries, degree of uncovering
- Differentiation stages—consist of clarification of differential and cohesive processes, group autonomy
- Separation—consists of a focus on evaluation, handling ambivalence, incorporating new resources

Interventive skills used during beginning work phase

The interventive skills the worker will use in the beginning work phase of a group are summarized below:
- Worker must tune into the needs and concerns of the members. Member cues may be subtle and difficult to detect.
- Seeking members' commitment to participate through engagement with members.
- Worker must continually asses:
  o Members' needs/concerns
  o Any ambivalence/resistance to work
  o Group processes

- o Emerging group structures
- o Individual patterns of interaction
- Facilitate the group's work.

Interventive skills used during middle phase

The interventive skills the worker will use in the middle phase of group work are summarized below:

- Being able to judge when work is being avoided.
- Being able to reach for opposites, ambiguities, and what is happening in the group when good and bad feelings are expressed.
- Supporting different ways in which members help each other.
- Being able to partialize larger problems into more manageable parts.
- Being able to generalize and find connections between small pieces of group expression and experience.
- Being able to facilitate purposeful communication that is invested with feelings.
- Identifying and communicating the need to work and recognizing when work is being accomplished by the group.

Methods of forestalling or dealing with termination

The group members' possible methods of forestalling or dealing with termination are described below:

- Simple denial—member may forget ending, act surprised, or feel "tricked" by termination
- Clustering—physically drawing together, also called super-cohesion
- Regression—reaction can be simple-to-complex. Earlier responses reemerge, outbursts of anger, recurrence of previous conflicts, fantasies of wanting to begin again, attempts to coerce the leader to remain, etc.
- Nihilistic flight—rejecting and rejection-provoking behavior
- Reenactment and review—recounting or reviewing earlier experiences in detail or actually repeating those experiences
- Evaluation—assessing meaning and worth of former experiences
- Positive flight—constructive movement toward self-weaning. Member finds new groups, etc.

Grief counseling

Grief counseling is short term and may utilize a variety of theoretical orientations derived from both communication theories and sociological concepts. Key tenets of this intervention approach include:

- Grief is a normal response at times of significant loss.
- Individuals typically pass through five stages of grief to reconcile a loss (Kübler-Ross, 1969):
    1. Denial, a defense mechanism that protects an individual from the full initial impact of the loss;
    2. Anger, at the irretrievability of the loss;
    3. Bargaining, considering all "what if" and "if only" elements that could have prevented or could restore (appeals to God, etc.) the loss;
    4. Despair/depression, as the full meaning of the loss emerges; and
    5. Acceptance, surrendering to loss and coming to believe in eventual recovery.

- Individuals must eventually pass through all grief stages (some more briefly than others) for recovery to occur, often repetitively engaging various stages at various times and in varying order according to their needs and coping capacity at the time.

Length of treatment

Extended periods of time for treatment are needed for those approaches that focus on personality change. Shorter-term treatment is called for in those approaches that focus on behavioral change, cognitive change, or problem solving. Examples are crisis intervention, task-centered treatment, cognitive, and behavioral treatment.

Views of treatment relationship

One view of the treatment relationship sees the therapeutic relationship as the main channel for promoting change and providing support. Another view sees the worker's role as ally, teacher, or coach. In this view, a here-and-now approach is taken. This can be seen in behavioral, cognitive, or crisis intervention models for practice.

Treatment planning

The treatment plan is used to set goals and objectives and to monitor progress. Goals are considered broad-based aims that are more general in nature (e.g., becoming less anxious, developing improved self-esteem), while objectives are the fundamental steps needed to accomplish the identified goals. Because objectives are used to operationalize goals, they must be written with considerable clarity and detail (questions of who, what, where, when, why, and how should be carefully answered). Properly constructed objectives must be based upon the client's perceptions of needs, as opposed to a clinician's bias, whenever possible. Finally, the treatment plan should be revised and updated as often as necessary to ensure that it remains an effective guiding and monitoring tool.

Maltreated/traumatized children

The treatment planning in social work practice with maltreated/traumatized children is explained as follows:
- Principal goal is protecting child from further harm and halting any further abuse, neglect, or sexual exploitation immediately and conclusively. This may require temporary or permanent removal of an offending caretaker or household member, or removal of the child from the home to a safe place.
- Secondary goal is creating conditions that insure that abuse or neglect does not recur after supervision/treatment is terminated. May include prosecution/incarceration of offending party. May include evaluation of non-offending parent's long-term capacity and motivation to protect the child.
- Official agency can and will use legal authority to insure compliance with agency directives when necessary. Worker should be aware that possibility of child's removal may be primary concern of parent and may lead to panic, dissembling, or flight.
- Treatment's goal is to help parents learn parenting/relational skills that can change parental behavior and child's responses.

Treatment plan for substance use disorder

The components of a treatment plan for a client with a substance use disorder are as follows:
- A strategy to achieve abstinence or to reduce the effects or use of substances.
- Efforts to increase ongoing compliance with the treatment program, prevent relapse, and enhance functioning.
- Clinical management.
- If necessary, additional treatments for clients with associated conditions.

Informed consent

Informed consent requires that no agreement to receive any treatment will be deemed valid unless sufficient information has been provided to achieve meaningful consent. The information provided should include the potential risks (both if treatment is refused and if treatment is provided) and the hoped-for benefits. The associated costs of treatment and available options for payment should be reviewed. While every remote potential eventuality and outcome cannot always be addressed, the information presented should include that which a "reasonable person" would expect in the presenting circumstances. Simply delivering information, however, is not sufficient to secure genuine informed consent. The client must also be helped to understand the information in language and with examples appropriate to his or her intellectual capacity, primary language and communication skills, and educational background. Where an individual lacks the capacity for consent (e.g., a minor, a developmentally delayed adult, a cognitively impaired frail elder, someone suffering from mental illness), informed consent from a legal guardian should be obtained.

Effective communication

Communication involves the conveying of information, whether verbally or nonverbally between individuals and has two key aspects: sending and receiving information. Each of these requires unique skills, and effective communication requires proficiency in both. Essential principles of communication include:
- All aspects of communication must be accounted for in any exchange
- Communication may be written, verbally spoken, or nonverbally delivered via body language, gestures, and expressions
- Not all communication is intentional, as unintentional information may also be conveyed
- All forms of communication have limits, further imposed by issues of perception, unique experiences, and interpretation
- Quality communication accounts for issues of age, gender, ethnicity/ culture, intellect, education, primary language, emotional state, and belief systems.
- Optimum communication is "active" (or "reflective"), using strategies such as: furthering responses (nodding, etc.); paraphrasing; rephrasing; clarification; encouragement ("tell me more"); partialization (reducing long ideas into manageable parts); summarization; feelings reflection; exploring silence; and, nonverbal support (eye contact, warm tone, neutral but warm expressions, etc.).

The following are key rules for quality communication with clients:
- Don't speak for the client; instead allow the client to fully express him or herself.
- Listen carefully and try diligently to understand.
- Don't talk when the client is speaking.
- Don't embellish; digest what the client has actually said, not what you presume was said.

- Don't interrupt, even if the process is slow or interspersed with long pauses.
- Don't judge, criticize, or intimidate when communicating.
- Facilitate communication with open-ended questions and a responsive and receptive posture.
- Avoid asking "Why" questions, which can be perceived as judgmental.
- Communicate using orderly, well-planned ideas, as opposed to rushed statements.
- Moderate the pace of your speech, and adjust your expressions to fit the client's education, intellect, and other unique features.
- Ask clarifying questions to enhance understanding.
- Attend to nonverbal communication (expression, body language, gestures, etc.).
- Limit closed-ended and leading questions.
- Avoid "stacked" (multi-part) questions that can be confusing.

Proper nonverbal communication

To facilitate the sharing process it is important for a social worker to present as warm, receptive, caring, and accepting of the client. However, the social worker should also endeavor not to bias, lead, or repress client expressions by an inappropriate use of nonverbal cues. Frowning, smiling, vigorous nodding, etc., may all lead clients to respond to the social workers' reactions rather than to disclose their genuine feelings and thoughts. To this end, a social worker will endeavor to make good eye contact, use a soft tone of voice, present as interested and engaged, etc., but without marked expressions that can influence the dialogue process. Sitting and facing the client (ideally without a desk or other obstruction in between), being professionally dressed and groomed, sitting close enough to be engaging but without invading another's "space," and using an open posture (arms comfortable in your lap or by your sides, rather than crossed over your chest) can all facilitate the communication process.

"Active" listening techniques

Active listening techniques include the use of paraphrasing in response, clarification of what was said to you, encouragement ("tell me more"), etc. Key overarching guidelines include:
1. Don't become preoccupied with specific "active listening strategies"; rather, concentrate on reducing client resistance to sharing, building trust, aiding the client in expanding his or her thoughts, and ensuring mutual understanding.
2. The greatest success occurs when a variety of active listening techniques are used during any given client meeting.
3. Focus on listening and finding ways to help the client to keep talking. Active listening skills will aid the client in expanding and clarifying his or her thoughts.
4. Remember that asking questions can often mean interrupting. Avoid questioning the client when he or she is midstream in thought and is sharing, unless the questions will further expand the sharing process.

Uninterrupted opportunities for clients to speak

There are many reasons to limit a client's opportunities to speak. Time may be inadequate, the workload may be impacted, the client may seem distracted or uninterested in sharing, etc. However, only by allowing the client to divulge his or her true feelings can the worker actually know and understand what the client believes, thinks, feels, and desires. Barriers to client sharing include:

1. Frequent interruptions: instead, you might jot a short note to prompt your question later;
2. Supplying client words: a client may seem to have great difficulty finding words to express his or her feelings and you may be tempted to assist. However, this may entirely circumvent true expression, as the client may simply say, "Yes, that's it," rather than working harder to find his or her true feelings;
3. Filling silence: long "pregnant pauses" can be awkward. You may wish to fill the silence, but in so doing you may prevent the client from finding thoughts to share.

Use of "leading questions"

Leading questions are those that predispose a particular response. For example, saying, "You do know that it is okay to ask questions, don't you?" is a strongly leading question. While it may seem an innocuous way to ensure that someone feels free to ask questions, it may not succeed in actually eliciting questions. Instead, ask the client directly, "What questions do you have?" This way of asking not only reveals that questions are acceptable, but is much more likely to encourage the client to openly share any confusion he or she is having. Even less forceful leading questions can induce a bias. For example, when a couple comes in for counseling, asking, "Do you want to sit over here?" could prevent you from seeing how they elect to arrange themselves in relation to you and each other (a very revealing element in the relationship). Instead, you might simply say, "Feel free to sit anywhere you'd like." Avoiding leading questions is an important skill in the communication process.

Terminating a treatment relationship

Ideally, termination occurs voluntarily and after all treatment goals have been met, though involuntary and precipitous terminations sometimes occur (e.g., because of moves, limited insurance coverage). Where possible, the social worker and the client should collaborate on identifying a termination date, based upon goal attainment, support needs, etc. Termination typically involves goal review, along with discussion about plans for steps the client can take to maintain the progress achieved and to continue progress in identified areas needing further development. Clinicians should be aware that impending termination can elicit varied client feelings, including sadness, anxiety, anger, rejection, and a sense of loss. Any such feelings should be thoroughly processed as a termination date approaches. Where overly intense client feelings arise, a follow-up meeting some weeks later may help. Regardless, the client should be reassured that he or she may return at any time, when this is feasible.

Similarities found among all approaches to social work practice

Three similarities that one can find among all different approaches to social work practice are as follows:
- All depend upon the use of worker-client relationship in some way.
- All use some form of assessment, treatment planning, and goal setting.
- All utilize a means of evaluating treatment.

Social work roles

Social workers may serve in many roles, including:
- Administrator: evaluating and developing policies and managing programs
- Advocate: defending, representing, and supporting vulnerable clients

- Broker: providing resource and service linkages to individuals in need
- Case manager: connecting, coordinating, and monitoring client services
- Counselor: exploring, treating, and resolving client, family, and/or group issues and problems
- Educator and teacher: researching and providing educational information, organizing and leading classes, teaching knowledge, skills, and/or behaviors that facilitate successful coping, growth, and relationships
- Policy maker, Lobbyist: working to identify, understand, and resolve problems in local communities or in society as a whole by garnering support from key interest groups to marshal and wield influence for positive and necessary change.

Core social work values and goals held by major social work theorists

Core values:
- Worth of the individual
- Right of individuals to access to services
- Right of individuals to fulfill potential without regard to class, race, gender, or sexual orientation
- Self determination
- Confidentiality

Goals are to help clients:
- Improve social functioning
- Resolve problems
- Achieve desired change
- Meet self-defined goals

Primary, secondary, and tertiary prevention

Primary, secondary, and tertiary prevention is discussed below:
- Primary prevention: intervention begun before any evidence of the onset of a problem (parent education programs are an example).
- Secondary prevention: early detection and treatment of a problem.
- Tertiary prevention: treatment in the acute phase of a problem.

Social policy and incremental change

Social policy is a collection of laws, regulations, customs, traditions, mores, folkways, values, beliefs, ideologies, roles, role expectations, occupations, organizations, and history—all focusing on the fulfillment of critical social functions. Incremental change takes place when small changes build on each other to slowly create larger change. An example of this in social policy is the passing of Medicare, which was later followed by the acceptance of Medicaid.

Research process

Research
Research is the process by which a hypothesis is either supported or rejected. A hypothesis is a statement of supposition either for or against a specific idea. Standardized processes of data collection explore the hypothesis in a valid, reliable, and replicable way. Research is either

qualitative or quantitative. Qualitative research is descriptive and explores an issue, group, or individual. It is inductive and relies largely on focus groups, in-depth interviews, and reviews. It tends to be unstructured, subjective, and non-statistical and addresses a problem or condition from the perspective experience. Because it is unstructured, the findings tend to be less generalizable to other groups or situations. It is often the first step in the formulation of a theory, preparatory to subsequent quantitative research. Quantitative research is deductive and relies on systematic data collection and analysis, using tools such as objective comparisons, measurements, experiments, and surveys. Because of the formalized, representative, and objective nature of quantitative research, the findings tend to be generalizable.

Common study designs

There are three common study designs: exploratory, descriptive, and experimental.

- An exploratory research design is common when little is known about a particular problem or issue. Its key feature is flexibility. The results comprise detailed descriptions of all observations made, arranged in some kind of order. Conclusions drawn include educated guesses or hypotheses.
- When the variables you choose have already been studied (e.g., in an exploratory study), further research requires a descriptive survey design. In this design, the variables are controlled partly by the situation and partly by the investigator, who chooses the sample. Proof of causality cannot be established, but the evidence may support causality.
- Experimental studies are highly controlled. Intervening and extraneous variables are eliminated, and independent variables are manipulated to measure effects in dependent variables (e.g., variables of interest)—either in the field or in a laboratory setting.

Data and findings are stored securely to protect confidentiality and prevent tampering.

Steps

The key steps in the research process are:

1. Problem or issue identification: including a literature review to further define the problem and to ensure that the problem has not already been studied
2. Hypothesis formulation: creating a clear statement of the problem or concern, worded in a way that it can be operationalized and measured
3. Operationalization: creating measurable variables that fully address the hypothesis
4. Study design selection: choosing a study design that will allow for the proper analysis of the data to be collected.

Single system experimental designs

Three common single system experimental designs are summarized below:

- The A-B-A design begins with data collection in the pre-intervention phase (A) and then continuously during the intervention phases (B). The intervention is then removed (returning to "A") and data are again collected. In this way an experimental process is produced (testing without, with, and then again without intervention). In this way, inferences regarding causality can be made, and two points of comparison are achieved. However, the ethics of removing a successful intervention leaves this study poorly recommended.
- The A-B-A-B study overcomes this failure by reintroducing the intervention ("B") at the close of the study. Greater causality inferences are obtained. However, even temporary removal of a successful intervention is problematic (especially if the client drops out at that time), and this design is fairly time-consuming.

- Therefore, the B-A-B design (the "intervention repeat design") drops the baseline phase and starts and ends with the intervention (important in crisis situations and where treatment delays are problematic), saving time and reducing ethical concerns.

The most basic single system design is the "A-B design." The baseline phase (A) has no intervention, followed by the intervention phase (B) with data collection. Typically, data are collected continuously through the intervention phase. Advantages of this design include
- Versatility
- Adaptability to many settings, program styles, and problems
- Clear comparative information between phases.

Single system research designs from a practice evaluation perspective

Evaluation of the efficacy and functionality of a practice is an important aspect of quality control and practice improvement. The most common approach to such an evaluation is the single system study approach. Selecting one client per system ($n = 1$), observations are made prior to, during, and following an intervention. The research steps are:
1. Selection of a problem for change (the "target")
2. Operationalizing the target (i.e., into measurable terms)
3. Following the target during the "baseline phase" (i.e., prior to the application of any intervention)
4. Observing the target and collecting data during the "intervention phase" (during which the intervention is carried out). There may be more than one phase of data collection.

Data that are repeatedly collected constitute a single system study "time series design." Single system designs provide a flexible and efficient way to evaluate virtually any type of practice.

Measures of variability

Measures of variability (or variation) include:
- The range, or the arithmetic difference between the largest and the smallest value (idiosyncratic "outliers" often excluded)
- The interquartile range, or the difference between the upper and lower quartiles (e.g., between the 75th and 25th percentiles)
- The standard deviation, or the average distance that numerical values are dispersed around the arithmetic mean.

Correlation refers to the strength of relatedness when a relationship exists between two or more numerical values, which, when assigned a numerical value, is the correlation coefficient (r). A perfect (1:1) correlation has an r value of 1.0, with decimal values indicating a lesser correlation as the correlation coefficient moves away from 1.0. The correlation may be either positive (with the values increasing or decreasing together) or negative (if the values are inverse and move opposite to each other).

Sampling

Four types of sampling techniques are described below:
1. Simple random sampling: any method of sampling wherein each subject selected from a population has an equal chance of being selected (e.g., drawing names from a hat).

2. Stratified random sampling: dividing a population into desired groups (age, income, etc.) and then using a simple random sample from each stratified group.
3. Cluster sampling: a technique used when natural groups are readily evident in a population (e.g., residents within each county in a state). The natural groups are then subjected to random sampling to obtain random members from each county. The best results occur when elements within clusters are internally heterogeneous and externally (between clusters) homogeneous, as the formation of natural clusters may introduce error and bias.
4. Systematic sampling: a systematic method of random sampling (e.g., randomly choosing a number n between 1 and 10—perhaps drawing the number from a hat) and then selecting every nth name in the phone book to obtain a study sample.

In sampling:
- A population is the total set of subjects sought for measurement by a researcher.
- A sample is a subset of subjects drawn from a population (as total population testing is usually not possible).
- A subject is a single unit of a population.
- Generalizability refers to the degree to which specific findings obtained can be applied to the total population.

Tests of statistical significance

Statistical tests presume the null hypothesis to be true and use the values derived from a test to calculate the likelihood of getting the same or better results under the conditions of the null hypothesis (referred to as the "observed probability" or "empirical probability," as opposed to the "theoretical probability"). Where this likelihood is very small, the null hypothesis is rejected. Traditionally, experimenters have defined a "small chance" at the 0.05 level (sometimes called the 5% level) or the 0.01 level (1% level). The Greek letter alpha (α) is used to indicate the significance level chosen. Where the observed or empirical probability is less than or equal to the selected alpha, the findings are said to be "statistically significant," and the research hypothesis would be accepted.

Three examples of tests of statistical significance are:
- The chi square test (a "nonparametric" test of significance), which assesses whether or not two samples are sufficiently different to conclude that the difference can be generalized to the larger population from which the samples were drawn. It provides the "degree of confidence" by which the research hypothesis can be accepted or rejected (measured on a scale from zero [impossibility] to one [certainty])
- A t-test, used to compare the arithmetic means of a given characteristic in two samples and to determine whether they are sufficiently different from each other to be statistically significant
- Analysis of variance, or ANOVA (also called the or "F test"), which is similar to the t-test. However, rather than simply comparing the means of two populations, it is used to determine whether or not statistically significant differences exist in multiple groups or samples.

Statistical error

Types of statistical error are:
- Type I error: rejecting the null hypothesis when it is true
- Type II error: accepting the null hypothesis when it is false and the research hypothesis is true (concluding that a difference, or "beta," doesn't exist when it does).

Selecting a study design

Key factors guiding the selection of a study design include:
- Standardization: whether or not data can be collected in an identical way from each participant (eliminating collection variation)
- Level of certainty: the study size needed to achieve statistical significance (determined via "power calculations")
- Resources: the availability of funding and other resources needed
- The time frame required
- The capacity of subjects to provide informed consent and ethics approval via Human Subjects Review Committees and Institutional Review Boards.

Case studies or predesigns

Three types of case study or predesigns are:
- Design A, an observational design with no intervention
- Design B, an intervention-only design without any baseline
- Design B-C, a "changes case study" design (where no baseline is recorded, a first intervention [B] is performed and then changed [C] and data are recorded).

A significant limitation, however, is that causation cannot be demonstrated.

Data analysis and reliability

In testing a hypothesis (the assertion that two variables are related), researchers look for correlations between variables (a change in one variable associated with a change in another, expressed in numerical values). The closer the correlation is to +1.0 or –1.0 (a perfect positive or negative correlation), the more meaningful the correlation. This, however, is not causality (change in one variable responsible for change in the other). Since all possible relationships between two variables cannot be tested (the variety approaches infinity), the "null hypothesis" is used (asserting that no relationship exists) with probability statistics that indicate the likelihood that the hypothesis is "null" (and must be rejected) or can be accepted. Indices of "reliability" and "validity" are also needed. Reliability refers to consistency of results (via test–retest evaluations, split-half testing [random assignment into two subgroups given the same intervention and then comparison of findings], or in interrater situations, where separate subjects' rating scores are compared to see if the correlations persist).

Data collection

Key points in data collection include:
- Data should ideally be collected close to the time of intervention (delays may result in variation from forgetfulness, rather than from the intervention process).

- Frequent data collection is ideal, but subject boredom or fatigue must be avoided as well. Thus, make the data collection process as easy as possible (electronic devices can sometimes help).
- Keep the data collection process short to increase subject responsiveness.
- Standardize recording procedures (collect data at the same time, place, and method to enhance ultimate data validity and reliability).
- Choose a collection method that fits the study well (observation, questionnaires, logs, diaries, surveys, rating scales, etc.) to optimize the data collection process and enhance the value of the data obtained.

Categories of measurement

The four different categories of measurement are:
- Nominal: used when two or more "named" variables exist (male/female, pass/fail, etc.)
- Ordinal: used when a hierarchy is present but when the distance between each value is not necessarily equal (e.g., first, second, third place)
- Interval: hierarchal values that are at equal distance from each other
- Ratio: one value divided by another, providing a relative association of one quantity in terms of the other (e.g., 50 is one half of 100).

Validity

Validity indicates the degree to which a study's results capture the actual characteristics of the features being measured. Reliable results may be consistent but invalid. However, valid results will always be reliable. Methods for testing validity include:
- Concurrent validity: comparing the results of studies that used different measurement instruments but targeted the same features
- Construct validity: the degree of agreement between a theoretical concept and the measurements obtained (as seen via the subcategories of (a) convergent validity, the degree of actual agreement on measures that should be theoretically related, and (b) discriminant validity, the lack of a relationship among measures which are theoretically not related)
- Content validity, comprising logical validity (i.e., whether reasoning indicates it is valid) and face validity (i.e., whether those involved concur that it appears valid)
- Predictive validity, concerning whether the measurement can be used to accurately extrapolate (predict) future outcomes.

Social services and social welfare services in the U.S

Social services endeavor to maintain quality of life in society and include social welfare (poverty and poor health prevention via "entitlements"), along with other government and privately operated programs, services, and resources. Types of social services include:
- Education
- Employment
- Health and medical services
- Housing
- Minimum income grants
- Nutrition
- Retirement
- Welfare (for children and the elderly)

Benefits include cash grants (e.g., unemployment, supplemental income) and "in kind" benefits (e.g., food stamps). Delivery systems include:

- Employment-based, obtained by or through employment (health insurance, retirement, and disability [both short and long term, including maternity and family leave])
- Government-based, consisting of tax relief, such as deductions (e.g., dependents, medical costs) at the local, state, or federal level
- Philanthropy-based, comprising programs for needy families, at-risk youth, etc.
- Personal contributions, such as child care, private health care, etc.
- Public-based, whereby not-for-profit agencies and public agencies provide services, such as shelters, adoption services, and disaster relief, free or at a reduced rate (sliding scale, etc.).

Public assistance programs in the U.S. for housing and health care

Public housing consists of government-built residential facilities that provide low-cost to no-cost rent for means-tested poor individuals and families. The Subsidized Housing Program offers federal funds to reduce rental costs for the means-tested poor and to aid in maintaining public residential facilities. Additional public housing assistance programs include home loan assistance programs, home maintenance assistance programs, and "Section 8" low-income reduced rent programs (rental vouchers). Medical assistance for the means-tested poor is covered primarily by the Medicaid program, managed by the individual states. Jointly funded by federal and state funds, the program was created in 1965 under Title XIX of the Social Security Act. The federal government imposes certain guidelines, around which the states establish eligibility standards, services, and rates, and provide overall administration. Medicaid is generally limited to means-tested families with children, recipients of SSI, foster care and adoption assistance recipients, infants born to women receiving Medicaid, children younger than age 6, and pregnant women in families living at or below 133% of the national poverty line.

TANF program and General Assistance

The Temporary Assistance for Needy Families (TANF) program replaced the Aid to Families with Dependent Children (AFDC) program. TANF was created by the 1996 Personal Responsibility and Work Opportunity Reconciliation Act (also known as welfare reform) and is a federally funded, state-administered block grant program. The focus is on moving recipients into the workforce and returning welfare to its intended temporary and transitional role. General Assistance (GA) refers to a variety of social welfare programs developed by state and local government to aid those unable to meet eligibility for federal assistance programs. Eligibility criteria vary from state to state (even region to region, in some areas). Because there is no mandate for GA programs, they do not exist in all states, though most states have created some form of safety net of this kind.

Social Security Disability, Worker's Compensation, and Supplemental Security Income

Individuals with a permanent disability severe enough to prevent them from becoming gainfully employed may qualify for Social Security Disability (SSD). The disabling condition must be expected to last for at least one year or to result in the individual's demise. Individuals who contract a job-related illness or who are injured in the course of their work are covered by the social insurance program known as Worker's Compensation. Injuries resulting from intoxication, gross negligence, or deliberate misconduct are not covered. Coverage varies from state to state for this federally mandated state-administered program. Funding is primarily employer based, though some states may supplement operation costs. Supplemental Security Income (SSI) is a federally funded program supplemented by the state. It ensures baseline cash income to bring means-tested recipients above the poverty line. Poor elderly, disabled, and blind persons are the primary recipients.

Eligibility criteria for social service programs

Eligibility for social services can be determined in many different ways. Three common methods include:
- Universal eligibility: open to all applicants
- Selective eligibility: specific criteria (age, dependent children, etc.) and often "means tested" (for income and resources) with sliding scale costs
- Exceptional eligibility: open only to individuals or groups with special needs (e.g., veterans, people with specific disabilities) and usually not means tested.

Social Security Act of 1935

The Social Security Act (SSA) of 1935 provided "old age survivor" benefits, with full coverage beginning at age 65. Full eligibility gradually increases to age 67 for those born in or after 1960. To be fully "vested," one must have 40 lifetime credits (earned at 4 credits per year). Reduced compensation may be available for those retiring earlier. Today, the program covers not only retirees, but those with certain permanent disabilities and the minor children of deceased beneficiaries, in certain situations. As an "insurance trust fund," the program was intended to be self-sustaining by all those who pay in.

Food and nutrition assistance programs

The available food and nutrition assistance programs in the U.S. are summarized below:
- SNAP (Supplemental Nutrition Assistance Program, previously food stamps): funds to purchase approved groceries, issued according to family size and income (selective eligibility, means-tested), state-administered and federally funded.
- WIC (Women, Infants, and Children): a means-tested, selective eligibility program providing assistance to pregnant women, mothers of infants up to 5 months old, breastfeeding mothers of infants up to 12 months old, and children under 5 years old. Subsidies are provided for specific nutritious foods (infant formula, eggs, etc.). The program is state administered and federally funded.
- School lunch programs: federally funded assistance to children in means-tested families.
- Elderly Nutrition Program: food assistance for needy persons over age 60 via local churches and community centers.
- Meals on Wheels: delivery of meals to means-tested individuals and families via this locally funded and administered program.

Medicare program

Medicare was established in 1965 and is now run by the Centers for Medicare and Medicaid Services. Coverage was initially instituted solely for those over age 65 but was expanded in 1973 to include the disabled. Eligibility criteria include an individual/spouse having worked for at least 10 years in Medicare-covered employment, and U.S. citizenship. Coverage may include up to four sections:

- Part A: hospital insurance (hospital care, skilled nursing home care, hospice, and home health care)
- Part B: medical insurance (doctor's services and outpatient hospital services, diagnostic tests, ambulance transport, some preventive care including mammography and Pap tests, and durable medical equipment and supplies)
- Part C: Medicare Advantage (MA), run by private companies to provide Part A and Part B benefits and, often, additional benefits such as vision, hearing, and health and wellness programs
- Part D: Medicare Advantage–Prescription Drug plans (MA-PD) that include prescription drug coverage.

Government funding and oversight of social service programs

Government programs are funded by income taxes and Social Security taxes. Income taxes are termed "progressive" because they increase as income increases. Taxes such as sales taxes and Social Security taxes are termed "regressive" because they are flat-rate taxes that offer non-proportional relief to those in low-income situations. Flat-rate tax reform efforts have continued to fall short primarily because of the loss of available deductions, in spite of proposals for tax elimination for the very poor. Dependent deductions can be crucial to low-income families, and home mortgage deductions are crucial for some homebuyers. A trend to privatization of government programs has increased in recent years (e.g., government oversight and funding of privately operated agencies). However, concerns about adequacy, availability, and accountability remain concerning.

Unemployment insurance and child welfare programs

Unemployment insurance is a benefit to prevent undue economic hardship, providing for individuals who become involuntarily and temporarily unemployed. To be eligible, an individual must be actively seeking gainful employment. Benefits include job-seeking assistance and cash payments in reduced proportion to the lost income. The benefits are time limited and once exhausted they cannot be obtained again unless a new episode of employment and job loss occurs. Originating with the Social Security Act of 1935, the program is federally mandated and state administered. Funding comes from employer taxes, distributed by the states to those needing assistance. A variety of child welfare services and programs have been created for the safety, care, and support of abused, disabled, homeless, and otherwise vulnerable children. Services include adoption and foster care. Agencies investigating abuse and securing out-of-home placement, if necessary, also exist, along with programs for family maintenance and reunification.

Role of administrators in an agency/organization

Basic administrative functions include:
- Human resource management: recruiting, interviewing, hiring, and firing, as well as orienting and reassigning employees within the organization
- Planning and delegation: ensuring that the organization's mission, goals, objectives, and policies are in place, appropriate, and effective, and delegating necessary tasks to achieve these ends
- Employee evaluations, reviews, and monitoring to ensure competency and efficiency

- Advocacy: horizontal interventions (between staff or across a department) and vertical interventions (between departments and hierarchical staff relationships to resolve conflicts and complaints
- Conflict resolution: acting as a mediator and a protector of the various parties involved, ensuring equitable outcomes that remain within the scope of the organization and its goals.

Relationship between case managers and direct service agency's staff

The goal of case management is to ensure that clients with multiple issues receive the comprehensive services and aid they need in a timely and effective manner. The case manager does not provide direct services; instead, the case manager connects the client to direct service providers. The case manager is responsible for all the services provided by the direct service agency engaged. Thus, the case manager and the agency staff need a close working relationship, to ensure that all client needs are being met. While all areas of health and human services use case managers, they are especially utilized for the mentally ill, the elderly, and the disabled, as well as in matters of child welfare. Having one case manager responsible for all the needs of a client provides the client with the one-on-one attention needed and prevents the client from falling between the cracks when many direct service people are involved.

Relationship of agency staff with board members

The board of directors oversees the development of policies by agency administrators, and the staff of the agency carries out the policies as approved. The board must hold the staff accountable for the implementation of the policies, because policy operationalization may utilize a variety of potential pathways. Administration evaluates the staff, and the performance of the staff ultimately reflects on the agency, which in turn reflects on the board. Representative staff members have the right to communicate with the board about any problems they face in implementing the policies. Open lines of communication between the board and the staff ensure success in the agency. The board, administration, and staff should have a triangular relationship based on clear job descriptions that state the responsibilities of each.

Financial and organizational status of not-for-profit agencies

Not-for-profit (nonprofit) entities operate, in many ways, similar to for-profit entities. However, there are some key differences:
- Not-for-profit organizations must not be structured to pursue commercial purposes (i.e., profiteering on goods and services sold to the public).
- Members of a not-for-profit organization may not personally benefit as shareholders or investors.
- Certain tax benefits can accrue to not-for-profit organizations, within parameters defined by the Internal Revenue Service, which are not available to for-profit entities.
- Finally, the goals of these organizations tend to be charitable in nature (e.g., caring for vulnerable populations), and they seek and receive funding primarily via government and philanthropic grants, as well as from gifts, donations, and fundraising events.

Board of directors

Selection and composition

The agency's mission and overall goals must be kept paramount when choosing board members. Members must be committed, honest, and able to invest their time and energy in the agency. Responsibilities must be discharged with personal expertise and through meaningful relationships within the community. Interpersonal skills are essential, as board members deal directly with the other members of the board, professionals at the agency, and the general public. Some boards require the representation of certain professions within the community (e.g., a banker), but all members must bring a particular expertise to the board. The agency's mission and the personal responsibilities of each board member should be understood, and a specific orientation experience should be provided to ensure this understanding. Terms are typically limited to three years, with the possibility of a second term for those making unique contributions. The terms should rotate to ensure that seasoned board members are always available.

Functions

The power and authority vested in a board of directors depends upon whether they are overseeing a private or public agency. Public agencies have board members that are largely advisory or administrative, with less direct authority than those overseeing private entities. In private agencies or voluntary organizations, the board is empowered to define the general path of the agency and to control all systems and programs operating under its auspices. The board is responsible to any sources that provide monetary contributions, to the community, to the government, and to all consumers that use the agency's programs. To be successful, members of a social service agency's board must have knowledge of all operations. The function of the board is to oversee the design of policies, develop short- and long-term planning, confirm the hiring of personnel, oversee general finances and financial expenditures, deal with the public, and be accountable for the actions of the agency.

Issues of communication that influence case consultation

Case consultation involves communication between a social worker and a direct service provider. The client could be an individual, family, or community. To be successful, consultation must have a purpose, a problem, and a process. The person requesting the consultation has the right to decline help, so the consultant must have high-value ideas to gain the trust of the consultee. An effective consultation process requires that the consultee determine the need for consultation and initiate the request for consultation, while the consultant and consultee must collaborate in assessing the problem, determine a plan for help, negotiate contracts, have a mutual list of objectives, determine the action to be taken, implement the plan, and measure and report the outcomes in a clear and concise manner. Communication is at the core of the process, so the consultant must have quality communication and problem-solving skills to be successful.

Linking and monitoring as core functions of case managers

Case managers must link clients with the service providers and resources needed, to the extent appropriate resources are available. Case managers are also responsible for helping clients overcome any obstacles in using the resources they are provided. When a client is unable to articulate his or her own needs, case managers must advocate and speak for them to get the assistance required. If necessary, help from an agency's administrative staff may be needed to fully address the services required. High-quality continuous monitoring is a key case management function. Good working relationships between case managers, clients, and direct service providers are essential to ensure a successful monitoring and accommodation process. Changes in plans and linkages may at times become necessary, as the client and/or available services may change and evolve.

Social work supervisor

As a middle manager, supervisors oversee direct service staff and report to administrative directors; they provide indirect client services (via direct service staff) and primarily serve the agency. Supervisory roles include:

- Recruitment and orientation
- Management: delegating duties, overseeing staff work, and resolving conflicts
- Education, training, and staff development: instructing staff regarding policies and procedures, and ensuring that training is available or pursued via in-service meetings, workshops, and continuing education courses
- Assessment and review: evaluating and providing feedback regarding staff performance
- Support: helping staff resolve issues and cope with stress and promoting a healthy work environment
- Advocacy: resolving complaints and pursuing necessary support for staff
- Role-modeling of quality practice, values, and ethics
- Program evaluator: ensuring that policies and procedures are effective and that staff adhere to guidelines.

Administration

Administration can be defined as follows:

- Means of managing organizations and all of their parts in order to maximize goals and have the organization succeed and grow
- Directing all the activities of an agency
- Organizing and bringing together all human and technical resources in order to meet the agency's goals
- Motivating and supervising work performed by individuals and groups in order to meet agency goals

Agency administration, structure, and management

All organizations should have a mission statement that sets forth the purpose, goals, and target service population of the organization. An organizational structure is then needed to pursue the delivery of services and achievement of the identified goals. An agency typically has three levels of bureaucratic staff: institution-wide leaders, management-level staff, and direct service providers. Typical social service agencies follow a classic Weberian bureaucratic model of organization. In a bureaucracy, leadership flows from the "top down," and tasks are rationally delegated to employees and departments best suited to achieve administrative and agency goals. Key characteristics of a bureaucracy include:

- Labor divided by functions and tasks according to specialized skills or a specific focus needed
- A hierarchical structure of authority
- Recruitment and hiring based upon an initial review of key qualifications and technical skills

- Rigid rules and procedures generally applied impartially throughout the organization and specifying employee benefits, duties, and rights
- Activities and responsibilities that are rationally planned to achieve overarching agency goals.

Relationships between administrators, supervisors, and supervisees

While all agency staff are concerned with providing quality services, administrators have a more external focus, while supervisors and direct service staff are focused internally. Administrators are charged with broad program planning, policy development, and ensuring agency funding, along with managing the agency's public image and community perceptions. By contrast, supervisors are more responsible for the implementation of policy and programs and ensuring staff adherence to those guidelines provided. New employees (during a probationary period) and those seeking licensure may engage in more formal supervision experiences. In the case of supervision for licensure, a written agreement will outline the goals, purpose, and scope of the supervision, along with meeting frequency and duration (to accrue required licensure hours), evaluations, whether or not sessions will be recorded (videotaped, etc.), and how feedback will be provided. Consultation and supervision differ, as consultation is an episodic, voluntary problem-solving process with someone having special expertise, in contrast to continuous and mandatory oversight with administrative authority.

Bureaucracy

Max Weber's characteristics of a bureaucracy are described below:
- Formal hierarchical structure.
- Written rules that delineate functions of the organization.
- Spheres of competence/organization by specialty
- Impersonal relationships
- Employment based on basis of competence
- Thorough and expert training.

Administration challenges unique to welfare organizations

Challenges unique to social welfare organizations in terms of administration are as follows:
- Clinical services can be difficult to assess objectively.
- Difficult to evaluate prevention programs as few techniques are able to measure events that have not occurred.
- Staff turnover due to low salary and burnout.
- Often dependent on political environment for funding.
- Can be difficult to implement systematization or routine work due to flexibility often required when dealing with human problems.

Power

Power is the ability to influence others in intended ways. Its sources include:
- Control of recourses
- Numbers of people
- Degree of social organization

Program evaluation

The following are the steps in program evaluation:
1. Determine what will be evaluated.
2. Identify who will be the consumer of the research.
3. Request the staff's cooperation.
4. Indicate what specific program objectives are.
5. Outline objectives of evaluation.
6. Choose variables.
7. Develop design of evaluation.
8. Apply evaluation design (conduct the evaluation).
9. Analyze and interpret findings.
10. Report results and put them into practice.

Inter-organizational relationships and social network analysis in community settings

Health care and social welfare fields often remain poorly integrated in larger community networks and systems. Social work agencies need to better coordinate and build partnerships to more fully meet the needs of their individual clients and the community at large. One barrier to interorganizational relationships is the allocation of resources, as funds for both health care and social services are limited. A related concern is the interpenetration of organizational boundaries, often established to preserve resources, the client base, etc. Consequently there is often conflict within and between agencies on how best to proceed to the next level of service and who will be primarily responsible, etc. One way to overcome past divisiveness is to have shared memberships in key planning processes, by which to map the flow of care from one level to the next. Further, always central to this process is the need to enhance how different agencies communicate with one another to provide cohesiveness and continuity.

Approaches for working with communities and larger systems

Social workers may be called upon to work for change and progress in large systems, such as in school districts, multi-site agencies, and communities and with governmental entities. In such situations, there are two key approaches: the *horizontal approach* and the *vertical approach* to engagement and intervention. The horizontal approach is used in working with centralized agencies and in communities. It involves bringing key participants (stakeholders) into the process of problem identification, consensus building, goal setting, and implementation and monitoring of an improvement process. The vertical approach is used when there is a need to reach outside or beyond the community or centralized entity environment. This approach involves learning about hierarchical levels of leadership in government, charitable organizations, grant-funding institutions, etc., and then collaborating with key leaders in problem identification, consensus building, goal setting, and program implementation and monitoring to achieve the necessary goals. An understanding of systems theory and eco-systems (or life model) theory can aid in this process.

Determining tactics for community organization practice

To determine the best tactics to use in community organization, consider the following factors:
- The degree of differences or commonality in the goals between the community group and the target system.
- The relative power of the target system and the community group.
- The relationship of the community group to the target system.

Collaborative tactics:
- Include problem solving, joint action, education, and mild persuasion.
- Require a perceived consensus in goals, power equality, relatively close relationships, and cooperation/sharing.

Campaign tactics:
- Include hard persuasion, political maneuvering, bargaining/negotiation, and mild coercion.
- Require perceived differences in goals, inequality in power, and intermediate relationships.

Contest tactics
- Include public conflict and pressure.
- Require public conflict, disagreement concerning goals, uncertain power, distant or hostile relationships.

Tasks/goals of community organization practice

The tasks/goals of community organization practice are as follows:
- Change public or private priorities in order to give attention to problems of inequality and social injustice.
- Promote legislative change or public funding allocation.
- Influence public opinions of social issues and problems.
- Improve community agencies/institutions in order to better satisfy needs of the community.
- Develop new ways to address community problems.
- Develop new services and coordinate existing ones.
- Improve community access to services.
- Set up new programs and services in response to new or changing needs.
- Develop the capacity of grassroots citizen groups to solve community problems and make claims on public resources for under-served communities.
- Seek justice for oppressed minorities.

Social-psychological aspect of community practice

There are several ways of understanding the social-psychological aspect of community.
- The belief that people of a community are bound together by an existing area of interest. They feel connected based on goals they share, needs, values and activities that makeup the feeling of community.
- The belief that there is a personal-psychological community within each individual. This is the view from one person that reflects what the community is like.
- Children and lower-class individuals tend to view community as having more narrow boundaries than the middle and upper class adults do.
- The cultural-anthropological view of community, which looks at community as a form of social living that is defined by attitudes, norms, customs, and behaviors of those living in the community.

Models of community organization practice

Models of community organization practice are summarized below:
- Locality Development model
  - Working in a neighborhood with the goal of improving the quality of community life through broad-spectrum participation at the local level.
  - Is process-oriented with a purpose of helping diverse elements of the community come together to resolve common problems and improve the community.
  - Tactics include consensus and capacity building. As the organization resolves smaller problems, it facilitates the solving of more complex and difficult problems.
  - The worker's roles include enabler, coordinator, educator, and broker.
- Social Planning model
  - Involves careful, rational study of a community's social, political, economic, and population characteristics in order to provide a basis for identifying agreed-upon problems and deciding on a range of solutions. Government organizations can be sponsors, participants, and recipients of information from social planners.
  - Focus on problem solving through fact gathering, rational action, and needs assessment.
  - Tactics may be consensus or conflict.
  - The worker's roles include researcher, reporter, data analyst, program planner, program implementer, and facilitator.
- Social Action model
  - This model requires an easily identifiable target and relatively clear, explainable goals. Typically, the target is a community institution that controls and allocates funds, community resources, and power and clients are those who lack social and economic power.
  - Assumption in this model is that different groups in the community have interests that are conflicting and are irreconcilable. In many cases, direct action is the only way to convince those with power to relinquish resources and power.
  - Tactics include conflict, confrontation, contest, and direct action.
  - The worker's roles include that of advocate, activist, and negotiator.
- Social Reform model
  - In collaborating with other organizations for the disadvantaged, the worker's role is to develop coalitions of various groups to pressure for change.
  - This model is a mixture of social action and social planning.
  - Strategies include fact gathering, publicity, lobbying, and political pressure.
  - Typically, this approach is pursued by elites on behalf of disadvantaged groups.

Differences between COP and other social work practice

Community organization practice (COP) substantially differs from other forms of social work practice (i.e., with groups and individuals) in the following ways:
- COP highlights knowledge about social power, social structure, social change, and social environments.
- COP acknowledges the reciprocal process between the individual and the social environment. It seeks to influence and change the social environment as it is seen as the source and likely solution for many problems.

- In the view of COP, social problems result from structural arrangements rather than from personal inadequacies. Consequently, resource and social power reallocation leads to changes in the community and eventually in individuals.

Important terms

Statistic — A statistic is a numerical representation of an identified characteristic of a subject.

Descriptive statistics — Descriptive statistics are mathematically derived values that represent characteristics identified in a group or population.

Inferential statistics — Inferential statistics are mathematical calculations that produce generalizations about a group or population from the numerical values of known characteristics.

Measures of central tendency — Measures of central tendency identify the relative degree to which certain characteristics in a population are grouped together. Such measures include:
- The mean, or the arithmetic average
- The median, or the numerical value above which 50% of the population is found and below which the other 50% is located
- The mode, or the most frequently appearing value (score) in a series of numerical values.

Professional Relationships, Values, and Ethics

Problematic treatment models for gays and lesbians

Problematic treatment models for practice with gays and lesbians are explained below:
- The moral model for treatment is religiously oriented and views homosexuality as sinful.
- The medical model in some forms views homosexuality as a mental illness.
- Reparative or conversion psychotherapy focuses on changing a person's sexual orientation to heterosexual. Traditional mental health disciplines view this type of treatment as unethical and as having no empirical base.

Community organization practice values

The following are the values of community organization practice:
- Working with, not for clients, and in so doing, enhancing their participatory skills.
- Developing leadership, particularly the ability to foresee and act on problems.
- Strengthening communities in order that they are better able to deal with future problems.
- Redistributing resources in order to enhance the resources of the disadvantaged.
- Planning changes in systematic and scientific ways.
- Rational problem-solving process: studying the problem, defining it, considering possible solutions, creating a plan, then implementing and evaluating the plan.
- Advancing the interests of the disadvantaged in order for them to have a voice in the process of distribution of social resources.

State mandates to report child abuse

Every state in the U.S. has laws that mandate that social workers report the mere suspicion of child abuse to the appropriate authorities. A good faith report gives the worker immunity from civil or criminal liability if the report is not verified as social workers cannot be found liable for following the law. Informing clients of the worker's decision to make a report is determined situationally, particularly if there is a concern of the client's violent reaction to self or others.

Concerns when reporting sexual abuse

Perpetrators of these crimes can be highly motivated to obtain retractions and may threaten or use violence to do so. A major concern in developing immediate and long term strategies for protection and treatment is the role of the non-abusing parent and his or her ability to protect the child. The victim may be safer if the worker does not notify the family when making the report. Great care must be taken by the worker with these cases.

Reporting client as danger to self or others

The circumstances under which a social worker must report that a client is a danger to self or others are described below:
- The client's mental state is such that he or she may deliberately or accidentally cause harm to self.

- The client makes a direct threat to harm another person and there is a reasonable possibility that he or she can carry out the threat.
- Duty to warn: All mental health professionals have a duty to warn individuals who are threatened. This principle was established by the Tarasoff Decision (*Tarasoff vs. Regents of University of California, 1976*).

Ethical considerations when selecting study design

The ethical issues/concerns involved with selecting a study design are as follows:
- Research must not lead to harming clients.
- Denying an intervention may amount to harm.
- Informed consent is essential.
- Confidentiality is required.

Social worker's ethical responsibilities to clients

A social worker's ethical responsibilities to clients include:
1. Keeping the client's interests paramount and promoting client well-being
2. Honoring and promoting client self-determination (limited only if client choices present a serious, foreseeable, and imminent risk of danger, to either the client or others)
3. Securing "informed consent," (i.e., ensuring that treatment choices are made only after all reasonably possible risks, benefits, burdens, costs, and options have been explained to and understood by the client)
4. Providing only those services in which the social worker is experienced, competent, an authorized by virtue of education, licensure, and/or certification
5. Providing culturally sensitive services
6. Avoiding conflicts of interest that may compromise judgment or bias services, even if termination is subsequently required
7. Not providing independent services to clients related to each other (e.g., couples, family members, etc.)
8. Avoiding multiple relationships with a client (e.g., counselor and fiduciary, conservator, etc.).
9. The preservation of client privacy (except where reportable abuse or threat of abuse, subpoena, referral, and/or cross-coverage otherwise requires)
10. Disclosing confidential information only when and to the extent required by law
11. Ensuring that clients have appropriate and timely access to their records
12. Scrupulously avoiding all inappropriate physical contact with clients (e.g., close hugging, kissing, overly familiar touching, sexual contact)
13. Providing clients with a relationship that is free from all sexual harassment
14. Setting fees with consideration for fairness and in the context of the client's ability to pay
15. Ensuring service continuity
16. Ensuring that services are terminated when the client no longer needs the services being provided.

Ethical obligations of supervisors

The NASW Code of Ethics addresses the ethical obligations of supervisors to their employees. Specifically:

- Social work supervisors should supervise and/or consult within only their area of expertise, knowledge, and competence.
- Supervisors are responsible for setting proper boundaries that are clear, culturally sensitive, and ethically sound.
- Social work supervisors should not accept multiple relationships with supervisees where potential harm, exploitation, or other untoward outcome could result (e.g., formalized personal counseling outside the scope of employment).
- All supervisee evaluations should be provided in a manner that is both fair and respectful.

Social worker's ethical responsibilities to colleagues

Social worker ethical responsibilities to colleagues, as defined by the Code of Ethics of the National Association of Social Workers (NASW) include:

- Ensuring that all colleagues are treated with respect
- Ensuring that any confidential information shared in the course of professional communication is also treated confidentially and with respect
- Obtaining consultation from colleagues when it is appropriate and necessary to serve the clients' best interests
- Recognizing colleagues' expertise and referring clients to colleagues when it would result in a client being better served
- Avoiding, as a supervisor, any sexual relations with and/or sexual harassment of any colleague under supervisory authority, including students and trainees, as well as formal employees
- Ensuring that any unethical conduct by colleagues is corrected, discouraged, or prevented or else exposed.

Purposes of NASW Code of Ethics

The NASW identifies six purposes of its Code of Ethics: (1) Identifying core values fundamental to social work's mission, (2) reflecting those core values through a summary of general principles and defining a group of more specific ethical standards for guidance in practicing social work, (3) helping social workers consider pertinent factors in the event of ethical dilemmas or conflicting obligations, (4) supplying ethical standards for the social work profession's accountability to the public, (5) acquainting new social workers with the discipline's values, mission, and ethical principles and standards, and (6) defining standards that the social work profession can apply to evaluate whether any social worker's conduct has been unethical. This enables the NASW to make decisions about adjudicating complaints filed against members alleging unethical conduct, for which the NASW has established formal procedures. Social workers who subscribe to the NASW Code of Ethics are required to participate in its adjudication proceedings and comply with any sanctions or disciplinary judgments informed by the code, as well as to cooperate in implementing it.

Core values

The core values of the social work profession, according to the NASW Code of Ethics, are as follows:
- Service
- Social justice
- Dignity and worth of the person
- Importance of human relationships
- Integrity
- Competence

Categories of ethical standards

The NASW identifies six ethical standards categories pertaining to all social workers' professional activities as ethical responsibilities related to the following: (1) to their clients, (2) to their colleagues, (3) in their practice settings, (4) as professionals, (5) to the profession of social work, and (6) to the wider society. Before briefly describing each of these identified standards, the NASW also points out that although some of these are guidelines for professional behavior, which can be enforced, others are "aspirational" and that persons responsible for reviewing alleged violations must use professional judgment to decide whether/to what degree a standard can be enforced.

Ethical responsibilities to clients

Commitment to clients
Under "Social Workers' Ethical Responsibilities to Clients," Standard 1.01 is "Commitment to Clients." This standard states that promoting client well-being is social workers' first responsibility, and client interests generally take precedence. It adds, however, that specific legal requirements or overall societal responsibility can sometimes override client loyalty—e.g., legally mandated reporting of child abuse or of threatening harm to others/self by clients—and that social workers must advise clients of this.

Client self-determination
Under the heading of "Social Workers' Ethical Responsibilities to Clients," the NASW Code of Ethics Standard 1.02 is entitled "Self-Determination." Self-determination refers to the autonomy of an individual to make decisions and take actions without the permission, influence, consultation, or advice of other people or groups. In this case, it refers to the self-determination of the clients of social workers. This ethical standard states that social workers should not only respect their clients' rights to self-determination, but they should also promote these rights; in addition, they should provide their clients with help in their endeavors toward identifying goals and/or making those goals clearer or more specific. Notwithstanding this ethical responsibility of the social worker to support self-determination in their clients, an additional caveat named in this ethical standard is the statement that if a social worker finds in his or her professional opinion that a client's actions or possible actions present imminent, serious, and anticipatable risk to others or self, the social worker can restrict some client rights to self-determination.

Informed consent
Social workers must obtain valid informed consent, as appropriate, for providing services to clients in professional relationships. They must inform clients in comprehensible, clear language of their services' purposes, related risks, limits, expenses, and alternatives; client rights to withdraw or refuse consent; and consent time limits. They must offer clients the chance to ask questions.

Assuring client comprehension includes providing interpreters and/or translators for ESL clients and detailed oral explanations for illiterate or low-literacy clients. Social workers should inform clients unable to give informed consent according to their comprehension levels, seek appropriate third-party permission, and assure that third-party actions are in clients' best interests and wishes. When clients are involuntarily receiving services, social workers should inform them of the degree to which they have a right to refuse services and of the extent and nature of those services. Social workers must inform clients of the risks and limitations related to providing services through electronic media. They should also secure informed consent from clients before videotaping, audiotaping, or allowing third-party observation of their services to clients.

Competence
In the NASW Code of Ethics, under Standard 1, "Social Workers' Ethical Responsibilities to Clients" Standard 1.04 is "Competence." Under this standard, the NASW advises that social workers should represent themselves as being competent and provide services only within the limits of their certification, licensure, training, education, supervised work experience, received consultations, and/or other pertinent professional credentials or experience. The NASW further enjoins social workers to deliver services or apply intervention approaches or techniques with which they are unfamiliar only after they have appropriately studied, consulted about, and been trained and supervised in these services by persons who are competent in those practices. In addition, this standard indicates that in any emergent field of professional social work practice wherein no standards have yet been established with general acceptance, social workers should use prudent judgment and obtain suitable training, education, supervision, consultation, and research; they should also take other responsible measures to assure that they protect their clients from being harmed and also to assure that their own work is competently carried out.

Cultural competence and social diversity
Standard 1, "Social Workers' Ethical Responsibilities to Clients," is the first standard area in the NASW Code of Ethics. Under this standard category, Standard 1.05 is entitled "Cultural Competence and Social Diversity." The first provision of this standard is that social workers should acknowledge the assets present in every culture and understand culture and the functions it serves in human society and behavior. The second provision is that social workers should know or learn about the cultures of all of their clients and have developed a "knowledge base" of these cultures and that, by providing services that are culturally sensitive and responsive to individual as well as cultural group differences, be able to demonstrate their cultural competence in service delivery. The third provision is that social workers should seek to understand, and pursue education in, the nature of oppression related to social diversity, including in race, color, ethnicity, national origin, sex, sexual orientation, gender identity/expression, age, religion, immigration status, marital status, political beliefs, and physical or mental disabilities.

Conflicts of interest
Under the NASW Code of Ethics first standards area, "Social Workers' Ethical Responsibilities to Clients," Standard 1.06 is "Conflicts of Interest." This standard includes the following: (a) vigilance to and avoidance of conflicts of interest impeding impartiality and professional discretion; informing clients of possible/real conflicts of interest; and taking reasonable actions to resolve these in clients' best interests, which can sometimes require professional relationship termination and indicated referral. (b) Never exploiting others or professional relationships unfairly to advance business, personal, political, or religious motives. (c) Avoiding dual/multiple relationships, concurrent or sequential, that risk client harm or exploitation; or, if such relationships are inevitable, taking measures for client protection and being responsible to establish culturally sensitive, appropriate, and clear boundaries. (d) In-service delivery to family members, couples, or

other related clients, clarifying their professional responsibilities to each individual and who are considered clients. Social workers anticipating conflicts of interest, e.g., when testifying in divorce proceedings, child custody cases, etc., should take suitable measures to limit conflicts of interest and clarify their roles with all those involved.

Privacy and confidentiality
The provisions of Standard 1.07, "Privacy and Confidentiality," are under Standard 1, "Social Workers' Ethical Responsibilities to Clients" of the NASW Code of Ethics. (a) Social workers respect client privacy rights; only request clients' private information essential for delivering services, evaluating social work, or conducting research; and protect private information confidentiality. (b) With valid client/legal designee consent, social workers may disclose confidential information when indicated. (c) Unless for "compelling" professional purposes, social workers must protect all confidential information procured during professional service. Preventing harm to clients/others is the exception necessitating disclosure. In this case, social workers only disclose directly pertinent information in the smallest amounts required for the indicated purposes. (d) To the degree possible, social workers inform clients in advance of disclosure and possible outcomes, regardless of whether through client consent or legal requirement. (e) As early as possible in professional relationships and as needed throughout, social workers discuss client confidentiality rights limits and confidentiality's nature with clients and involved others and review instances wherein disclosure may be requested or legally required. (f) When serving groups/families/couples, social workers pursue group agreement regarding individual confidentiality rights and responsibilities to protect others' information and inform participants that they cannot guarantee every individual's compliance.

(g) When conducting group, family, marital, or couples counseling, a social worker should inform these clients of the social worker's own policy, as well their employer's and his or her agency's policy, regarding disclosure by the social worker of confidential client information among the involved individuals. (h) Social workers must not disclose confidential information to third-party payers without client authorization. (i) Social workers should never discuss confidential information in public, semipublic, or any other settings without ensuring privacy. This includes restaurants, waiting rooms, elevators, and hallways. (j) Social workers will protect client confidentiality as lawfully allowed during legal proceedings. If a court or other legally authorized entity orders disclosure of privileged or confidential information without client consent and that disclosure could cause client harm, social workers are advised to request that the court withdraw such orders, keep records sealed against public view, or limit those orders as narrowly as possible. (k) Social workers must protect client confidentiality when responding to requests from reporters or other members of the press or the media.

(l) Social workers must protect the confidentiality of all written and electronic client records and other sensitive information. This protection includes taking reasonable measures to assure that confidential client records are stored in a secure place and preventing access or availability of client records to others who are not authorized to access them. (m) Social workers are enjoined to avoid disclosing identifying client information whenever possible. They should take precautions to keep information electronically transmitted to others confidential. (n) Social workers should dispose of and transfer client records so they protect client confidentiality, while also complying with state regulations of both social work licensure and records management. (o) Social workers must protect client confidentiality through reasonable precautions in case of the social worker's death, incapacitation, or termination of practice. (p) Social workers should never disclose identifying client information for training/teaching reasons without client consent. (q) Social workers should never disclose identifying client information to consultants without client consent or "compelling need." (r) Social workers must also protect deceased clients' confidentiality following these standards.

Client access to records

Under Standard 1, "Social Workers' Ethical Responsibilities to Clients," Standard 1.08, "Access to Records," provides guidelines for social workers regarding client access to the records a social worker keeps about that client. First, the standard indicates social workers should give their clients "reasonable" access to records of client history, referrals, and the counseling relationship, sessions, and interactions, etc. However, it also states that if a social worker has reason to believe that records access has the potential to cause the client harm or cause a serious misunderstanding, the social worker should help the client interpret the records and consult with the client about them. Nevertheless, it advises social workers only to limit client access to their records or parts of them in "exceptional" cases of "compelling" evidence that serious client harm would ensue from records access. Social workers should document in client records any client records access requests and social worker rationales for withholding any records information. They should also protect confidentiality for others discussed or identified in client records when providing access.

Sexual relationships with clients

NASW Code of Ethics Standard 1, "Social Workers' Ethical Responsibilities to Clients," includes Standard 1.09, "Sexual Relationships." Its first two provisions indicate the following: (a) Under no circumstances should a social worker ever engage in sexual activities or any kind of sexual contact with clients whom they currently serve. This applies not just to forced contact, but also to consensual contact. (b) Social workers must also avoid sexual activity or contact with relatives, close friends, or others having close personal relationships with their clients whenever any harm to or risk of exploitation of the client could possibly ensue from such contact. Because it can interfere with maintaining the professional counseling relationship and its applicable boundaries, sexual contact or activity with individuals personally close to the client has the ability to cause the client harm. Moreover, it is not the client or the client's relatives or others in close personal relationships with the client who are responsible for establishing culturally sensitive, appropriate, and clear boundaries—it is the social worker.

Code Standard 1, "Social Workers' Ethical Responsibilities to Clients," addresses sexual relationships in Standard 1.09, "Sexual Relationships." The third guideline under this standard says (c) because it has the potential for causing harm to their clients, social workers must avoid sexual activity or sexual contact, not only with current clients (a) and with those close to current clients (b), but also with former clients. An additional provision within this guideline is that if a social worker claims "extraordinary circumstances" can justify any exception to this rule, that social worker—never the former client—is fully responsible to demonstrate that he or she has not intentionally or unintentionally coerced, manipulated, or exploited the former client. The fourth guideline under this standard says (d) just as a social worker's sexual contact with former clients can cause the client harm and interfere with professional boundaries, conversely, so can delivering clinical services to former sexual partners. Therefore, social workers should not accept individuals with whom they have previously had sexual relationships as their clients.

Physical contact, sexual harassment, and derogatory language

Under Standard 1, "Social Workers' Ethical Responsibilities to Clients," of the NASW Code of Ethics, Standard 1.10 is entitled "Physical Contact." It states that social workers should refrain from making physical contact with their clients whenever such contact has any potential for causing psychological harm to the client. As examples, it identifies "cradling or caressing clients." When social workers engage in physical contact with clients appropriately—for example, when some specific therapeutic approaches include certain forms of physical contact or when some kinds of contact are found instrumental for building and/or maintaining rapport, trust, and the counseling relationship rather than inhibiting or damaging these—social workers have the responsibility to establish culturally sensitive, appropriate, and clear boundaries regulating that contact. Standard 1.11, "Sexual Harassment," prohibits social workers from requesting sexual favors, making sexual solicitations or sexual advances, or other sexually related physical or verbal conduct, all included as sexually harassing clients. Standard 1.12, "Derogatory Language," proscribes social workers' using disparaging words in oral or written communications about/to clients and prescribes respectful, accurate communications.

Payment for services

Under Standard 1, "Social Workers' Ethical Responsibilities to Clients," Standard 1.13, "Payment for Services," directs social workers to set fees that are commensurate with services provided, to ensure that fees are reasonable and fair, and to consider the client's ability to pay. It additionally warns social workers not to trade professional services for goods or services from clients as payment. The reason is that inappropriate relationship boundaries, exploitation, and conflicts of interest are all potential outcomes of bartering, especially with services. Conditions for exploring and possibly engaging in barter are "only in very limited circumstances" if it is shown that the client has initiated the arrangement and given informed consent and it is found essential to service provision, an accepted practice among local professionals, and freely negotiated without coercion. If accepting goods or services as payment from clients, social workers are fully responsible to demonstrate that the arrangement will not harm the client or counseling relationship. Also, when clients are entitled to services through the social worker's agency or employer, the social worker must not solicit private fees or other compensation.

Standards 1.14, 1.15, and 1.16 in NASW Code of Ethics

Standard 1 of the NASW Code of Ethics is entitled "Social Workers' Ethical Responsibilities to Clients." Under this standards area, Standard 1.14 is entitled "Clients Who Lack Decision-Making Capacity." It states that social workers should take "reasonable" measures to protect the rights and interests of clients whenever their professional roles include acting on behalf of clients who do not have the capacity for making informed decisions. Making informed decisions would include giving informed consent, which is addressed separately in more detail under Standard 1.03, "Informed Consent." Standard 1.15 is entitled "Interruption of Services." It states that in cases when professional services are interrupted by death, disability, illness, relocation, or unavailability, the social worker should make "reasonable efforts" to provide for continuity of services. Standard 1.16 is entitled "Termination of Services." This standard has six provisions. The first is that when professional relationships with and services to clients are no longer needed or they no longer meet client needs or interests, social workers should terminate those services.

The NASW Code of Ethics entitles its first standard as "Social Workers' Ethical Responsibilities to Clients." Under this category, Standard 1.16 is entitled "Termination of Services" and includes six provisions. The fourth of these six provisions is that a social worker should not terminate his or her professional services to a client in order to engage in a sexual, financial, or social relationship with that client. The fifth of these provisions is that if a social worker anticipates that his or her services will be interrupted or terminated, he or she should promptly inform his or her clients of this. In addition, the social worker should pursue the referral, transfer, or continuation of services, depending on the needs and preferences of the clients. The sixth and last provision is that if a social worker will be departing from a particular setting, the social worker should provide clients with suitable options, plus information about the risks and benefits of those options, for the continuation of services they have been receiving.

Ethical responsibilities to colleagues

Respect
In the NASW Code of Ethics, among six main areas of standards, Standard 2 is entitled "Social Workers' Ethical Responsibilities to Colleagues." In this category, the first ethical standard is 2.01, "Respect." It states first that social workers should show respect in their treatment of colleagues. This includes fairly and accurately representing their duties, perspectives, and qualifications. Second, it advises that social workers ought to refrain from making unjustified criticisms of their colleagues when communicating with other professionals or with clients. Such unfounded criticism can encompass casting aspersions on a colleague's degree of professional competence or on personal characteristics including race, color, ethnicity, national origin, immigration status, sex, sexual orientation, gender expression or gender identity, age, religion, marital status, political beliefs, and physical or mental disabilities. Third, this ethical standard gives the guidance to NASW members that a social worker should cooperate, not only with other social workers, but also with colleagues who work in related and other professions, whenever their cooperation will contribute to client well-being.

Confidentiality and interdisciplinary collaboration
Under Standard 2, "Social Workers' Ethical Responsibilities to Colleagues," NASW Code of Ethics Standard 2.02 is entitled "Confidentiality." It states that when their colleagues share confidential information in their professional interactions and relationships, social workers should respect its privacy. It also advises social workers to make sure that these colleagues understand how social workers are obligated to respect confidentiality and any associated exceptions. Standard 2.03, entitled "Interdisciplinary Collaboration," states that when social workers participate as members of interdisciplinary teams, they should make use of the social work profession's values, experiences, and perspectives to take part in and make contributions to decisions that affect client well-being. It adds that the ethical and professional responsibilities, of the individual team members and the group, should be defined clearly. Another provision of this ethical standard is that if a team decision triggers ethical considerations for a participating social worker, he or she should try to use indicated channels for resolution, and if this fails, to seek other means compatible with client well-being for addressing them.

Disputes involving colleagues
In the NASW Code of Ethics under Standard 2, "Social Workers' Ethical Responsibilities to Colleagues," Standard 2.04 is entitled "Disputes Involving Colleagues." This ethical standard includes two provisions: one relating to disputes between or among a social worker's colleagues and another relating to clients in terms of disputes that the social worker may have with his or her colleagues and/or to disputes that the social worker's colleagues may have between or among themselves. Provision (a) advises that when a social worker knows that a colleague and the colleague's employer are having a dispute, the social worker should not exploit this situation to obtain a position—for example, one that becomes available through the colleague's resignation, dismissal, or demotion—or to further the social worker's own interests otherwise. Provision (b) warns social workers not to take advantage of their clients in any disputes the social worker has with colleagues and not to involve clients in any improper conversations about their disputes with colleagues or about other social workers' disputes.

Consultation
Standard 2, entitled "Social Workers' Ethical Responsibilities to Colleagues," of the NASW's Code of Ethics includes Standard 2.05, which is entitled "Consultation." The first provision of this ethical

standard states that whenever it is in the best interests of their clients, social workers should avail themselves of the counsel and advice of their colleagues. The second provision of this ethical standard advises that social workers are obligated to obtain current information with regard to the competencies and areas of expertise of their colleagues before requesting consultations from them. By staying informed, social workers can determine which other professionals can best advise them and offer the most relevant, up-to-date, and accurate opinions and information. This provision also cautions that social workers should only ask for consultation from those colleagues who have demonstrated their knowledge, competence, and expertise regarding the topic of the consultation. The third provision warns social workers to be careful to disclose the smallest amounts of information needed for consultation purposes when they consult about their clients with colleagues.

Referral for services
The NASW Code of Ethics addresses referrals under Standard 2, "Social Workers' Ethical Responsibilities to Colleagues," in Standard 2.06, entitled "Referral for Services." The first provision of this standard is that whenever a social worker believes that he or she is not achieving reasonable progress or not being effective with a client and additional services are needed or another professional's specialized expertise or knowledge is required to serve the client's needs fully, the social worker should refer the client. The second provision enjoins social workers who refer clients to others also to take suitable measures to transfer the responsibility for providing services in an organized fashion. Ensuring that the transfer is an orderly process is important to promote the continuity of care. This provision also advises that social workers referring clients to other service providers first obtain client consent and then disclose all relevant information to those professionals. The third provision prohibits social workers from receiving or giving payment for referrals if the referring social worker did not provide any professional service.

Sexual relationships and sexual harassment
Standard 2, "Social Workers' Ethical Responsibilities to Colleagues," includes two ethical standards addressing sexual involvement. Ethical standard 2.07, "Sexual Relationships," in its first provision, warns social workers who serve as educators and/or supervisors not to involve themselves in sexual contact or activity with students, supervisees, trainees, or other colleagues when they wield professional authority over them. This ethical standard also cautions in its second provision that anytime a conflict of interest is a possibility, social workers should eschew involvement in sexual relationships with colleagues. This provision states in addition that if a social worker does become engaged in a sexual relationship with a colleague, or even anticipates that this will occur, then that social worker has the responsibility to transfer professional duties as needed to prevent such a conflict of interest. Standard 2.08, "Sexual Harassment," prohibits social workers from engaging in any physical or verbal behavior that is sexual in nature, including sexual solicitations, advances, or requests for sexual favors involving their colleagues, students, supervisees, or trainees.

Impairment
The NASW Code of Ethics addresses social workers' interactions with colleagues under Standard 2, "Social Workers' Ethical Responsibilities to Colleagues." In this area, Standard 2.09, entitled "Impairment of Colleagues," addresses the issue of impairment. The first provision of this ethical standard offers the guidance that if a social worker knows directly (i.e., not through third parties or hearsay) that another social work professional's effectiveness in professional practice is being impaired by mental health problems, substance abuse disorders, psychosocial distress, or personal problems, then the social worker with that knowledge should consult with the colleague whenever possible and help him or her to take actions to remediate the cause(s) of the impairment. The second provision follows up on the first one: If a social worker believes that impairment is

- 87 -

interfering with a colleague's effectiveness in practice and also believes the colleague has not taken sufficient measures to address this, the social worker should take action through proper avenues offered by NASW, other professional organizations, regulatory or licensing entities, agencies, and employers.

<u>Incompetence</u>
Among six main areas, NASW Standard 2 addresses "Social Workers' Ethical Responsibilities to Colleagues." Under this area, Standard 2.10 is entitled "Incompetence of Colleagues." A social worker may be incompetent for various reasons, including lack of adequate professional education; lack of sufficient training; lack of continuing education or professional development resulting in not keeping current in the field; lack of sufficient work experience; inappropriate behaviors; or inherent deficits in interpersonal skills, communication skills, intelligence, sound judgment, common sense, and/or other requirements of the profession despite having the proper education, preparation, training, and experience. This standard advises social workers having direct knowledge of incompetence in a social work colleague first to consult with the colleague when possible and to give the colleague assistance in taking action to remediate the incompetence. This standard also tells social workers who believe that another social worker is incompetent and has not taken sufficient action to address this, to take action themselves through proper channels that NASW, other professional organizations, their employers, agencies, and regulatory and licensing entities have established.

<u>Unethical conduct of colleagues</u>
Interactions with colleagues are addressed under NASW Code of Ethics Standard 2, "Social Workers' Ethical Responsibilities to Colleagues." Standard 2.11, "Unethical Conduct of Colleagues," first directs social workers to take sufficient steps to prevent, discourage, reveal, and correct any unethical conduct by their colleagues that they observe. It also says social workers should have knowledge of accepted policies and procedures for addressing ethics complaints on the federal, state, and local levels. This knowledge includes not only laws, statutes, and regulations, but also policies and procedures established by NASW, other professional organizations, regulatory and licensure groups, agencies, and employers. If a social worker believes a colleague has behaved unethically, this standard says that he or she should first discuss this with the colleague when possible, if productive dialogue is probable. It further advises that when needed, social workers finding colleague actions unethical should also act by contacting a state regulatory agency, licensure board, NASW inquiry committee, another professional ethics group, or through other applicable formal channels. This ethical standard also recommends helping and defending colleagues wrongfully accused of unethical behavior.

Ethical responsibilities in practice settings

<u>Supervision and consultation</u>
The NASW Code of Ethics Standard 3 is entitled "Social Workers' Ethical Responsibilities in Practice Settings." Its first Standard is 3.01, "Supervision and Consultation." The first provision of this ethical standard states that when social workers supervise others or consult with others, they must possess the knowledge and skills required for properly supervising or consulting and that when they do, they should perform these activities solely within the limits of their knowledge and competencies. The second provision of this ethical standard informs social workers that when they perform supervision or consultation, they have the responsibility of establishing culturally sensitive, appropriate, and clearly defined boundaries within the supervisory or consultative interaction or relationship. The third provision issues a warning to social workers who supervise others to avoid engaging in any dual or multiple relationships with supervisees if there is any

possibility of harm to the supervisee or a possibility of risk for exploitation of the supervisee. The fourth provision enjoins supervising social workers to show respect and fairness in evaluating supervisee performance.

Education and training

The third of the NASW six main standards areas in its Code of Ethics is Standard 3, "Social Workers' Ethical Responsibilities in Practice Settings." Standard 3.02 is entitled "Education and Training." This standard contains four provisions. The first provision of this ethical standard provides the guidance that when a social worker serves as a trainer, a field instructor, or any other kind of an educator of social work students, that social worker should deliver instruction that has as its basis the most up-to-date knowledge and information available within the social work profession. In addition, this provision advises social workers to deliver instruction only in areas in which they are knowledgeable and competent enough to teach them. The second provision of four within this ethical standard enjoins social workers who work as field instructors or educators of social work students to apply respect and fairness in the ways in which they conduct performance evaluations of the work that their students do during or after instructing them.

Client records

NASW's Code of Ethics addresses this topic under Standard 3, "Social Workers' Ethical Responsibilities in Practice Settings," with Standard 3.04, "Client Records." The first provision of this ethical standard enjoins social workers to take reasonable measures to assure that documentation reflects the provided services and is otherwise accurate in clients' records. The second provision of this ethical standard reminds social workers to provide documentation in records that is both timely and sufficient for facilitating current service delivery and for assuring continuity in future services provided to clients. The third provision in this ethical standard informs social workers that the documentation they furnish in client records should only include information related directly to the delivery of services to the client in order to protect the client's privacy to the degree that is proper and feasible. The fourth provision in this ethical standard instructs social workers to enable reasonable access to client records after service termination, including storing and maintaining records for the durations specified by pertinent contracts or state statutes.

Billing and client transfer

Standard 3, "Social Workers' Ethical Responsibilities in Practice Settings," of the NASW Code of Ethics includes Standard 3.05, "Billing." It states that social workers are expected to set and sustain practices in billing that identify the individual who provided services in the practice setting and that reflect accurately the extent and nature of services provided. Ethical standard 3.06 is entitled "Client Transfer." Its first provision addresses situations wherein clients receiving services from colleagues or other agencies contact a social worker seeking services. It advises that before agreeing to provide services, the social worker should consider the requesting client's needs carefully. To prevent or limit potential conflict and/or confusion, the social worker should discuss with prospective clients the nature of the existing service relationship and potential risks, benefits, and other implications of establishing a relationship with a new practitioner. The second provision recommends that when applicable, the social worker should discuss with a new client whether or not it is in the client's best interests for the social worker to consult with his or her previous service provider(s).

Administration

Under Standard 3, "Social Workers' Ethical Responsibilities in Practice Settings," Standard 3.07 is entitled "Administration." The first provision of this ethical standard advises social work administrators advocate for required resources inside and outside their agencies for meeting client needs. Its second provision directs social workers to advocate for fair, open resource allocation procedures. This includes developing a nondiscriminatory procedure founded on suitable principles and applied consistently for resource allocation when it is impossible to meet all client needs with the resources available. In its third provision, this ethical standard requires that social worker administrators should take reasonable actions to make sure that sufficient organizational or agency resources are made available for furnishing proper supervision of staff members. The fourth provision of this ethical standard advises social work administrators to take reasonable measures for assuring that the work environment under their responsibility is compliant with the NASW Code of Ethics; it promotes employee compliance with the Code of Ethics; and it advises for removing any organizational conditions impeding, violating, or discouraging this compliance.

Continuing education and staff development and commitment to employers
"Social Workers' Ethical Responsibilities in Practice Settings" is Standard 3 of the NASW Code of Ethics. Standard 3.08, entitled "Continuing Education and Staff Development," advises social work administrators and supervisors to take realistic actions to obtain or offer, for all staff under their responsibility, ongoing development and education that cover current information and emergent developments associated with social work ethics and practice. Ethical standard 3.09 is entitled "Commitments to Employers." It contains seven provisions. The first of these provisions states that, in general, social workers should fulfill the commitments they make to their employing organizations or agencies and employers. The second of these provisions requires that social workers should endeavor to improve the effectiveness and efficiency of the services they provide, and social workers should also work to improve the policies and procedures of their employing agencies. The third of the seven provisions enjoins social workers to act reasonably to assure their employers have awareness of social workers' ethical responsibilities as defined in the NASW Code of Ethics and also of what these responsibilities imply for practicing social work.

Commitments to employers
The NASW Code of Ethics addresses this general area in Standard 3, "Social Workers' Ethical Responsibilities in Practice Settings." Standard 3.09, entitled "Commitments to Employers," has seven provisions. The fourth provision offers social workers the guidance that they should not permit any interference with their ethical social work practices by any administrative orders, regulations, policies, or procedures issued by their employing organizations. This provision moreover advises social workers to engage in reasonable actions to assure that their employing organization's practices comply with the NASW Code of Ethics. The fifth provision adds the recommendation that social workers actively work to eliminate and prevent discrimination in employment policies and practices and work assignments issued by their employing organizations. The sixth provision advises social workers to identify and select only organizations applying fair personnel practices to assign student field experience placements and accept employment. The seventh and last provision of this ethical standard prescribes diligent stewardship of employing organization resources by social workers, including never using funds for unintended reasons, never misappropriating funds, and conserving funds appropriately and judiciously.

Labor-management disputes
Standard 3 of the NASW Code of Ethics' six standards areas is entitled "Social Workers' Ethical Responsibilities in Practice Settings," and it includes Standard 3.10, entitled "Labor-Management Disputes." The first provision of this ethical standard states that social workers are ethically able to participate in organized actions for the purpose of enhancing working conditions and client services in the social work profession. Participation includes forming and joining labor unions and participating in their activities. The second provision specifically addresses disputes between labor

unions and employer management personnel. It points out that the ethical principles, ethical standards, and values of the social work profession should guide all actions of social workers engaged in labor strikes, job actions, or labor-management disputes. Although conceding that social workers have "reasonable differences of opinion" about the priorities of their professional duties during job actions, labor strikes, or strike threats, this provision also guides them to analyze pertinent issues and their potential effects on clients carefully before they decide what they will do.

Ethical responsibilities as professionals

Competence

In the NASW Code of Ethics, Standard 4 is entitled "Social Workers' Ethical Responsibilities as Professionals." The first ethical standard in this area is 4.01, entitled "Competence." Its first provision states that the basis for social workers to accept employment or responsibilities should be only their current competence as is required or their intention of obtaining it. The second provision of this ethical standard urges social workers to endeavor to attain and maintain proficiency in professional practice and professional function performance. It advises social workers to stay up to date with emergent information related to social work and to examine this information critically. This provision also prescribes that social workers engage in continuing education that pertains to the practice of social work and social work ethics and that they review the professional social work literature routinely. The third provision of this ethical standard informs social workers that their practices should be based upon accepted knowledge that is applicable to social work and social work ethics. This knowledge includes empirically derived findings.

Discrimination; private conduct; and dishonesty, fraud, and deception

Although other areas of the NASW Code of Ethics also indirectly address discrimination, e.g., ensuring comprehension through interpretation/translation to surmount language or literacy barriers for informed consent (Standard 1.03), avoiding discrimination by learning about and seeking to understand social diversity and oppression (Standard 1.05), not voicing discriminatory comments to colleagues as a matter of respect (Standard 2.01) or they directly advise eradicating and preventing discrimination (Standard 6.04); under Standard 4, "Social Workers' Ethical Responsibilities as Professionals," Standard 4.02 is specifically entitled "Discrimination," and it prohibits practicing, enabling, allowing, or participating in any kind of discrimination based on race, color, ethnicity, national origin, immigration status, age, marital status, sex, sexual orientation, gender expression or identity, religion, political belief, or physical or mental disabilities. Standard 4.03, "Private Conduct," states that social workers must not allow their private behaviors to impede their capacities to discharge their professional duties. Standard 4.04, "Dishonesty, Fraud, and Deception," prohibits social workers from associating with, allowing, or participating in any fraudulent, dishonest, or deceptive practices.

Impairment

The NASW Code of Ethics addresses the ethical professional behavior of social workers under Standard 4, "Social Workers' Ethical Responsibilities as Professionals." This area includes Standard 4.05, titled "Impairment." Although social workers' responsibilities regarding impairment in colleagues is covered by Standard 2.09, "Impairment of Colleagues" under Standard 2, "Social Workers' Ethical Responsibilities to Colleagues," Standard 4.05 focuses on social workers' ethical responsibilities related to their own impairment. The first provision of this standard warns social workers not to permit their professional performance and judgment, or the best interests of clients or others for whom they are professionally responsible, to be compromised by their own mental health, substance abuse, psychosocial, legal, or personal problems. The second provision in this ethical standard advises that if social workers' personal, psychosocial, legal, mental health, or substance abuse problems do impede their professional performance and judgment, they should promptly request consultation and take whatever remedial steps are needed to protect clients and others by modifying workloads, terminating practice, and/or pursuing professional help.

Misrepresentation

Standard 4, "Social Workers' Ethical Responsibilities as Professionals," in the NASW Code of Ethics contains Standard 4.06, "Misrepresentation." Within this ethical standard, the first provision guides social workers to distinguish clearly between what they say and what they do as representatives of the social work profession, professional social work organizations, or their employing agencies versus what they say and do as private individuals. The second provision of this ethical standard prescribes that social workers correctly represent the authorized and official positions of professional social work organizations when they are speaking on behalf of these organizations. Under this ethical standard, the third provision is that when social workers represent their own professional credentials, qualifications, competence, education, and affiliations; the services they provide; or the outcomes they intend their services to attain, they must assure the accuracy of these representations. In addition, this provision enjoins social workers to claim only the pertinent professional credentials that they really have and moreover to correct any misrepresentations or inaccurate representations made by others regarding those credentials.

Solicitations and acknowledging credit

Prospective clients of social workers often encounter a variety of challenges, which renders them vulnerable to being coerced, manipulated, or unduly influenced. Therefore, the NASW Code of Ethics provides in Standard 4.07, entitled "Solicitations," under Standard 4, "Social Workers' Ethical Responsibilities as Professionals," that social workers should refrain from making any unrequested solicitation of these individuals. This ethical standard includes a second provision that, in addition, social workers should keep from soliciting clients for their consent to use the clients' past statements as testimonial endorsements. This provision also proscribes social workers from soliciting testimonial endorsements directly from current or previous clients and also from other individuals who are more susceptible than normal to being unduly influenced owing to their specific situations or circumstances. Standard 4.08, "Acknowledging Credit," provides that social workers should only take credit and responsibility as contributors, authors, or performers of work they have really contributed to or done. It also provides that social workers should acknowledge other people's work and contributions honestly.

Ethical responsibilities to the social work profession

Integrity of the profession

Standard 5 of the NASW Code of Ethics is entitled "Social Workers' Ethical Responsibilities to the Social Work Profession." Within this standards area, Standard 5.01 is entitled "Integrity of the Profession." The first provision of this ethical standard states that social workers should work to promote high standards of practice in their profession and to maintain them. The second provision of this ethical standard is that social workers should not only uphold, but also further, the mission, values, ethics, and knowledge of their profession. It also recommends that social workers should engage in suitable research, study, responsible criticism of their profession and active discussion about it to protect the integrity of the profession and to improve upon this integrity as well. The third of five provisions within this ethical standard gives the advice that social workers should make contributions of their professional expertise and their time to activities that further the respect of others for the integrity, competence, and value of the profession of social work.

In its third of five provisions, Standard 5.01, entitled Integrity of the "Profession," under Standard 5, "Social Workers' Ethical Responsibilities to the Social Work Profession" of the NASW Code of Ethics, recommends that social workers should contribute to activities advancing respect for the social work profession's competence, value, and integrity. It also offers several examples of such activities to accomplish this goal. These include participating in professional social work organizations, making presentations in their communities, giving testimony before legislative committees, conducting research in their field, providing consultations to other professionals in social work and related disciplines, providing services, and teaching. The fourth provision is for social workers to share their knowledge with colleagues and to contribute to the social work profession's knowledge base relative to its ethics, research, and practice. These include sharing knowledge at professional conferences and meetings and contributing to the profession's research literature. The fifth provision of this ethical standard enjoins social workers to take actions to prevent any unqualified and/or unauthorized social work practice.

Evaluation and research
"Social Workers' Ethical Responsibilities to the Social Work Profession" is the title of Standard 5 among six main standards areas in the NASW Code of Ethics. Standard 5.02, "Evaluation and Research," contains 16 provisions. Provision (a) is that all social workers should evaluate and monitor practice interventions, program implementation, and policies. Provision (b) is that social workers should contribute to the development of knowledge by facilitating and promoting research and evaluation. Provision (c) says that social workers should use evidence from research and evaluation fully in their professional practices, stay up to date about emergent knowledge pertinent to social work, and critically examine that knowledge. Provision (d) advises all social workers to consult institutional review boards as is indicated, to adhere to guidelines that have been established in order to protect the participants in their research and evaluation, and to consider with care all the potential consequences of the research or evaluation that they conduct or in which they are involved.

Provision (e) enjoins social workers who are conducting evaluations or research to procure written, voluntary, informed consent as is indicated from those who will be participating. Obtaining such consent is further defined in this provision as requiring social workers not to induce individuals unduly to participate and not to suggest or actually engage in penalizing or depriving them for refusing to participate. Social workers are also reminded to procure this consent with due respect for the privacy, dignity, and well-being of the participants. The benefits, risks, duration, extent, and nature of the participation is information that social workers should disclose when requesting informed consent. Provision (f) addresses participants incapable of providing informed consent. In these cases, social workers should give prospective participants suitable explanations, obtain whatever consent they are capable of understanding and giving, and then procure official written consent from authorized proxies.

Provision (g) prohibits social workers from conducting and/or designing evaluation or research without consent procedures (e.g., some archival research or naturalistic observation) unless justified by responsible, rigorous review for its educational, scientific, or applied value and unless equally efficacious alternatives with consent are impracticable. Provision (h) requires social workers to notify participants of their right to withdraw from research or evaluation without penalties at any time. Provision (i) accords social workers responsibility for assuring that participants have the indicated support services available. Provision (j) advises social workers to protect evaluation and research participants against undue mental and/or physical deprivation, distress, danger, or harm. Provision (k) limits social workers' evaluating services to discussing gathered information only with concerned professionals and only for professional purposes.

Provision (l) enjoins social workers to assure participants and their data confidentiality or anonymity. This includes informing participants of confidentiality measures and limits and times for any destruction of research data records.

Provision (m) says that unless formal, voluntary, written, informed consent has first been secured authorizing disclosure, social workers should leave out personally identifying information of participants in evaluation and research when they report results, to protect participants' confidentiality. Provision (n) requires social workers to accurately report all research and evaluation results. It cautions them not to falsify or fabricate any findings, and if errors are found in data after publication, to use standard publication procedures to correct these. Provision (o) warns social workers conducting research or evaluation to be vigilant for, and prevent, dual or multiple relationships with participants and to prevent conflicts of interest. It also advises social workers that if a possible or actual conflict of interest emerges, they should notify participants and take actions to resolve it with participant interests as the priority. Provision (p) instructs social workers to educate themselves, their colleagues, and their students regarding responsible research practices.

Ethical responsibilities to the broader society

Social welfare, public participation, and public emergencies
NASW Code of Ethics Standard 6, "Social Workers' Ethical Responsibilities to the Broader Society," contains four specific ethical standards. The first is Standard 6.01, "Social Welfare." It states the belief that all social workers ought to work to foster "the general welfare of society." This includes societal welfare on the local, state, national, and global levels, and it also refers to the development of human environments, communities, groups, and individual people. In order to realize social justice, this ethical standard says that social workers are responsible for supporting cultural, social, economic, and political institutions and values that are congruent with this aim. It also holds social workers responsible for helping to meet fundamental human needs through advocating for living conditions that further this goal. Standard 6.02, "Public Participation," recommends that social workers ought to shape social institutions and policies to facilitate informed public participation. Standard 6.03, "Public Emergencies," states that in the event of public emergencies, social workers should supply appropriate professional services as much as is possible.

Social and political action
Within Standard 6, "Social Workers' Ethical Responsibilities to the Broader Society" of the NASW Code of Ethics, Standard 6.04, "Social and Political Action," includes four provisions. The first of these provides that in order for all people to fulfill their fundamental human needs and also achieve full development, social workers have the responsibility of taking social and political actions that promote assuring that everybody has equal access to the opportunities, resources, services, and employment that they need. In addition, this provision advises social workers to be aware of how their practices are affected by political factors. It also recommends that pursuant to this awareness, social workers ought to promote social justice and fulfill fundamental human needs by advocating for changes in legislation and policy that enable the improvement of social conditions toward these ends. The second provision in this ethical standard makes the recommendation that social workers accord especial attention to oppressed, exploited, disadvantaged, and vulnerable groups and individuals and do this as part of taking actions that extend opportunities and choices for all people.

NASW Code of Ethics Standard 6, "Social Workers' Ethical Responsibilities to the Broader Society," includes Standard 6.04, "Social and Political Action," as its last ethical standard. Among four provisions, the third states that the responsibilities of social workers to contribute to respect for social and cultural diversity, in America and worldwide, by furthering conditions conducive to such respect. This provision also avers that social workers are responsible for supporting the increase of cultural resources and knowledge; advocating for institutions demonstrating culturally competent practices; supporting practices and policies respecting differences among people; and furthering policies that affirm social justice and equity for, and protect the rights of, all people. The fourth provision in this ethical standard prescribes that social workers are expected to engage in actions that eradicate and/or prevent anyone from exploiting, dominating, and/or discriminating against any class, group, or individual based on race, color, ethnicity, national origin, immigration status, age, marital status, sex, sexual orientation, gender expression or identity, religion, political belief, or physical or mental disabilities.

Ethical responsibilities

Social workers have ethical responsibilities due to their profession, including:
- Ensuring that high practice standards are maintained and promoted
- Sustaining, promoting, and preserving the profession's mission, ethics, knowledge, and values
- Pursuing and promoting research and evaluation that will contribute to the development and knowledge of the profession
- Examining and following the programs and policies in social work practice to ensure that they not only are effective but also properly promote the aims and mission of social work.

Social work ethical responsibilities to society include:
- Ensuring that the profession promotes society's general welfare
- Pursuing equal access to all resources by all individuals through relevant social and political activities
- Facilitating social and cultural diversity by supporting and promoting conditions receptive to these special concerns.

Social worker ethical responsibilities in practice settings include:
- Accepting supervisor or educator duties only if properly qualified
- Avoiding multiple relationships with students and supervisees
- Ensuring proper documentation in client records; (4) billing accurately and only for services rendered
- Advocating for clients that lack adequate resources and/or services
- Ensuring that continuing education is available and that staff development is provided to all staff.

Professional ethical responsibilities include:
- Possessing or promptly pursuing the necessary skills for any employment or assignment accepted
- Ensuring continuing proficiency in professional practice via ongoing education and learning
- Avoiding all discrimination against any individuals and groups
- Ensuring that professional practice is not encumbered by personal problems and issues
- Avoiding any solicitation of vulnerable individuals to become clients.

Confidentiality

Social work privilege does not have the same force as that of attorneys and clergy. Unlike clergy and attorneys, social workers may be compelled to testify in court under certain circumstances. Organizational policies should reflect the expectation of confidentiality:
- Records must be secured and locked.
- Policies should be in place that ensure that records not be left where unauthorized persons are able to read them.
- Computerized records should be secured with the same attention given to written records (hard copies).
- Agencies must provide spaces that permit private conversations so that conversations about clients can be held where they cannot be overheard.

Confidentiality if social worker is sued for malpractice

A worker who is sued for malpractice may reveal information discussed by clients. The worker should aim to limit the discussion of the content of clinical discussions to those statements needed to support an effective defense.

Confidentiality issues regarding indiscriminate sexual behavior or drug-paraphernalia sharing in a client who is HIV positive

The duty to protect as derived from the *Tarasoff* case has been rigorously debated in terms of other mechanisms of harm—for example, how to handle a situation where a client is HIV positive and is known to be having unprotected sex with a victim who is not aware of the client's HIV-positive status. Given the deadly nature of the sexually and blood-to-blood transmitted human immunodeficiency virus, it has been determined that a social worker or other clinician may be warranted in breaching confidentiality if education about the dangers and efforts at counseling have failed to alter the HIV-positive client's behavior. However, the following five specific criteria must be met:
1. The client must be known to be HIV positive.
2. The client must be engaging in unprotected sex or sharing drug injection paraphernalia.
3. The behavior must actually be unsafe.
4. The client must indicate intent to continue the behavior even after counseling regarding potential harm.
5. HIV transmission must be likely to occur.

HIPAA and the NASW confidentiality policies

In 1996 the federal government passed legislation providing privacy protection for personal health information. Known as HIPAA, this act:
- Places privacy protections on personal health information and specifically limits the purposes for its use and the circumstances for its disclosure
- Provides individuals with specific rights to access their records
- Ensures that individuals will be notified about privacy practices. The act applies only to "covered entities," which are defined as health care providers (physicians and allied health care providers), clearinghouses for health care services, and health plans.

The NASW has issued a policy on confidentiality. It provides general guidelines, including a client's right to be told of records being maintained and verification of the records for accuracy. It does not, however, specify how individuals may access these records.

Persons bound by confidentiality

All social workers, supervisors, administrators, clerical and administrative staff, volunteers, and trainees privy to client information are bound by rules of confidentiality.
Confidentiality exceptions include:
- Subpoena, but information released should be only as specifically ordered, arguments regarding relevance and scope may be useful, and a claim of "privileged communication" may be upheld, depending upon the case
- Treatment continuity, where vacation or leave by the practitioner, illness coverage, etc., may require other staff to view a client's file or to discuss the case
- Insurance coverage, which typically requires release of the DSM diagnosis and certain information regarding treatment progress, and the treatment contract the client signs should stipulate this, for liability purposes
- Client request of release of information to any third party, if by written request
- Mandated reporting, as previously addressed
- Child welfare, where information regarding abuse, harming of self or others, and legal violations must be disclosed to a parent or guardian, and the child should be told this at the outset of the relationship.

Right to privacy

Every individual has a right to expect that personal information disclosed in a clinical setting, including data such as their address, telephone number, Social Security number, financial information, and health information will not be disclosed to others, and no preconditions need be fulfilled to claim this right. The 1974 Federal Privacy Act (PL 93-579) also stipulates that clients be informed:
- When records about them are being maintained
- That they can access, correct, and copy these records
- That the records are to be used only for the purpose of obtaining absent written consent otherwise.

Exceptions are:
- Need-to-know sharing with other agency employees
- Use for research if identifying information is omitted
- Release to the government for law enforcement purposes
- Responding to a subpoena
- In emergencies, where the health and safety of an individual is at risk. While the law applies only to agencies receiving federal funds, many state and local entities have adopted these standards.

Informed consent

A client may provide consent for the worker to share information with family members, or with other professionals or agencies for purposes of referral. When the client provides this consent, he or she has reason to expect that shared information is in his or her best interest, and designed to improve his or her situation.

Liability

Liability for social workers is as follows:
- Clients can sue social workers for malpractice.
- The chain of liability extends from the individual worker to supervisory personnel to the director and then to the board of directors of a nonprofit agency.
- Most agencies carry malpractice insurance, which usually protects individual workers, however, workers may also carry personal liability and malpractice insurance.
- Supervisors can be named as parties in a malpractice suit as they share vicarious liability for the activities of their supervisees.

A client may allege and sue on grounds of malpractice at any time he or she deems that unprofessional conduct or improper treatment has occurred. In a solo practice, the social worker bears the brunt of this action alone. In an agency setting, liability extends downward from the board of directors to the agency direction to the relevant supervisor, and then to the practicing social worker. Because the costs of such litigation may be high, most agencies carry malpractice insurance, though it can be prudent for agency social workers to carry their own independent policies.

Vicarious liability (also called "imputed negligence" and "respondeat superior") refers to the liability of administrators and supervisors for the actions of those they oversee. If a social worker's conduct is within the scope of employment (even if acting away from the agency) the employer is primarily responsible (though personal liability may still accrue). To this end, supervisors and administrators must be familiar with the case loads and expertise of those they supervise.

Appropriate boundaries in the social worker-client relationship

In social worker–client relationships, the following principles apply:
- The Code of Ethics should guide proper professional boundaries.
- It is never proper to pursue or allow nonprofessional, social, recreational, or personal relationships with clients. Cite the Code of Ethics, if necessary, to avoid communicating rejection.
- Any gift, beyond a small token, should be politely and thoughtfully declined, citing the professional Code of Ethics, if necessary.
- Intimate relationships between social workers and clients (whether sexual or just overly close) are never appropriate. If a social worker develops unexpected feelings, supervisory consultation should be sought to evaluate the situation and consider assigning an alternate social worker. Those in private practice may need to refer the client to another clinician.
- Confidentiality is a bedrock principle, and care should be taken to preserve it—with exceptions limited to reportable abuse (including credible threats to the client or others), court subpoena, case transfer, or limited cross coverage.

General rights for clients

General rights for social work clients are as follows:
- Confidentiality and privacy
- Informed consent
- Access to services (if service requirements cannot be met, a referral should be offered)
- Access to records (adequately protective but not onerously burdensome policies for client access to services should be developed and put in place)
- Participation in the development of treatment plans (client cooperation in the treatment process is essential to success)
- Options for alternative services/referrals (clients should always be offered options whenever they are available)
- Right to refuse services (clients have a right to refuse services that are not court ordered; ethical issues exist when involuntary treatment is provided, but mandates do not allow options other than referrals to other sources of the mandated service)
- Termination by the client (clients have a right to terminate services at any time and for any reason they deem adequate, except in certain court-ordered situations).

Obligations for social work administrators

The Code of Ethics is as applicable to administrators as to primary service providers. Specifically:
- Maintaining the pertinence of advocacy for clients' needs, applied at the intra- and interagency level of planning and resource allocation
- Ensuring that resource and service allocations are based on consistent principles and are not discriminatory in any way
- Making sure that proper supervision is available for necessary staff oversight
- Ensuring that the NASW Code of Ethics is supported and applied in the work setting, and removing any barriers to full compliance that may exist
- Providing or arranging for the provision of continuing education and staff development and ensuring staff release time for these purposes.

Lesser eligibility

This concept asserts that welfare payments should not be higher than the lowest paying job in society and derives from Elizabethan Poor Law. It suggests that economic and wage issues underlie the size of benefits and the availability of welfare. Some believe it is a way to control labor and maintain incentives for workers to accept low-paying or undesirable jobs that they might otherwise reject.

Mission and core values of social work

The National Association of Social Workers (NASW) describes the mission of social work as being the enhancement of human well-being and assisting individuals to secure their basic human needs in society. The professional focus of social work is on the individual in the context of society and the social and environmental forces involved in the problems of everyday life. The Code of Ethics identifies certain professional core values, which include:

- Competence
- Human relationships
- Individual dignity
- Integrity
- Service
- Social justice.

Client

A "client" is the focus of intervention, treatment, advocacy, support, etc., and could be an individual, family, group, community, or organization. The mission of social workers is to promote growth, well-being, and social justice on behalf of their clients.

Practice Test

Practice Questions

1. For about three weeks, Josie's gums have been swollen. She is drooling and frequently crying. She occasionally runs a slight fever. She seems most content when chewing a chilled plastic gel-filled ring. What age group is Josie MOST likely to be in?
   a. 0–4 months
   b. 4–8 months
   c. 8–12 months
   d. 12–24 months

2. What is a common indicator of infant development in the first year of life?
   a. growth of the arms and legs
   b. frequency of smiling
   c. amount eaten
   d. development of the head

3. According to Piaget's model of childhood development, at which age is the principle of conservation LEAST likely to be present?
   a. 6 years
   b. 7 years
   c. 8 years
   d. 9 years

4. What conditions are MOST commonly associated with the neural tube (birth) defect spina bifida?
   a. mental retardation, paralysis, and hydrocephalus
   b. microcephaly and blindness
   c. blindness and deafness
   d. dwarfism

5. What therapeutic intervention is generally thought to be the best approach to reactive attachment disorder?
   a. teaching the child how to acknowledge his or her caregivers
   b. getting the father more involved in parenting
   c. working with the caregiver on his or her self-image
   d. working with the caregiver's reactions to his or her child

6. In Erikson's eight-stage model of psychosocial development, which stage could be negatively affected by inappropriate toilet training, leading to an "anal-retentive" or "anal-expressive" personality type later in life?
   a. trust versus mistrust
   b. autonomy versus shame
   c. initiation versus guilt
   d. industry versus inferiority

7. Freud's theory of the Oedipus conflict gave rise to what theoretical construct?
    a. inferiority complex
    b. penis envy
    c. castration anxiety
    d. erectile dysfunction

8. Which chemical is known as the one that accompanies bonding behavior between mothers and children and between lovers?
    a. serotonin
    b. dopamine
    c. oxytocin
    d. oxycontin

9. A couple who has been dating off and on are arguing about commitment, and the man says, "You said you didn't want any strings—because you don't want any responsibilities!" The woman counters—"No, I didn't: You said you didn't want any strings." The video of the earlier session shows that what the woman said is right. Which defense mechanism is the man using?
    a. rationalization
    b. substitution
    c. reaction formation
    d. projection

10. A family therapist asks the daughter to place other members of her family in positions that she feels demonstrates their current relationships to each other. The daughter places the mother and son very close together, with the teenage son's hand leaning on his mother's shoulder. She places her father at the door, with his hand on the doorknob, but facing his wife. Finally, she puts herself in a chair at the far end of the room, as if she is observing the others, but not part of the group. In this sculpting technique, what is the client MOST likely saying about her family?
    a. She is demonstrating a family secret.
    b. She is showing enmeshment between mother and son.
    c. She is showing this family's low cohesion.
    d. She is showing her lack of attachment.

11. Which of Maslow's hierarchy of needs is MOST likely to encompass spiritual development in an individual's lifespan?
    a. esteem
    b. self-actualization
    c. love and belonging
    d. safety

12. Harry's mother is extremely concerned that her son is not crawling at 7 months of age, because "all the other children in his playgroup are." She wants to have him evaluated for a disability, despite the fact that in every other way, his development is quite normal. What is the FIRST thing the caseworker should suggest?
    a. a medical evaluation
    b. play therapy
    c. waiting another 90 days to see what happens
    d. therapy for his anxious mother

13. Which characteristic is LEAST likely to be associated with teenage behavior?
    a. black-and-white thinking
    b. mood swings
    c. lack of experimentation
    d. concern with appearance

14. What is the LEAST likely outcome for a young adult who becomes a parent in late adolescence?
    a. underemployment
    b. lower educational achievement
    c. higher financial achievement
    d. lack of a stable intimate relationship

15. In midlife, Erikson's stage of generativity (versus stagnation) takes place when
    a. a family has children
    b. an individual stays in lucrative work that makes him or her unhappy
    c. a couple gets divorced
    d. an individual feels motivated and optimistic about contributing

16. Simon is 66 years old and was recently ordered by the court to attend counseling for an outburst in a grocery store, where he threw a can of pop at the clerk for being too slow in ringing up his purchases. His wife attends the first session as well, and although he insists his memory is "as good as it ever was," she shakes her head. He seems distracted and angry; she placates him, but he lashes out verbally. When the caseworker asks her if anything has changed recently, she tells him that Simon has always been a good-natured, easygoing man, but that lately he has been "difficult." As they are leaving, Simon, looking puzzled, says, "I don't even know why we're here."

What is the FIRST possible diagnosis a caseworker would consider in this case?
    a. alcoholism
    b. Alzheimer's disease
    c. bipolar disorder
    d. impulse-control disorder

17. Which behavior is MOST likely to indicate secure attachment of a child to the primary caregiver?
    a. checking the whereabouts and attitude of the primary caregiver when encountering a stranger
    b. accepting treats from strangers
    c. sitting on a stranger's lap
    d. not asking for or responding to comfort from a caregiver

18. According to Maslow's hierarchy of needs, which one of the following is the MOST basic human need?
    a. the need to be married
    b. the need for financial security
    c. the need for food
    d. the need for respect

19. Which is NOT considered a personal protective factor in helping clients increase their resiliency?
    a. problem solving
    b. goal setting
    c. competition
    d. success in life tasks

20. John has been trying to come out as gay for months, but his mother refuses to accept his sexual identity. Even after he told her, "I don't want a girlfriend, Mom, I like guys," she arranged a blind date for him with the daughter of her friend. When he tried again in family counseling, he said, "Mom, I'm gay." His mother instantly replied, "No you're not. You're just confused."

Which defense mechanism is John's mother using?
    a. projection
    b. refusal
    c. denial
    d. reaction formation

21. Which theorist coined the term "inferiority complex"?
    a. Alfred Adler
    b. Sigmund Freud
    c. Carl Jung
    d. Erik Erikson

22. Jeanette has recently left her unhappy marriage and her job. She is not sure what to do next, and she even feels unsure about her decision to divorce because her father and mother believe she is making a mistake. They tell her she shouldn't expect "too much happiness" from a marriage, and she feels that by ending it, she is disappointing them. What is the MOST likely name for Jeanette's current condition?
    a. identity disorder
    b. identified patient
    c. identity crisis
    d. enmeshment

23. Tuckman's 1965 model of small-group work labeled four stages, and in 1977, he proposed a fifth stage, which was
    a. storming
    b. conforming
    c. adjourning
    d. performing

24. What is the MOST important thing for a social worker to do in the first session with a family?
    a. identify the primary problem
    b. join with each member
    c. establish his or her professional credibility
    d. set boundaries

25. A young man with autism shows swift improvement when he is paired with a horse and starts learning to ride. His parents remove him from the program, citing an inability to drive him to the stables, and they refuse to allow the social worker to provide alternative transportation. The man speedily reverts to his self-harming behaviors and has to be hospitalized. From a systems standpoint, what is the MOST likely explanation for his parents' decision?
    a. They simply could not provide the needed transportation.
    b. Systems cannot tolerate change.
    c. The parents were protecting their son from outside influences.
    d. The parents were unconsciously reestablishing the homeostasis of their system.

26. An agency obtains funding for additional programming in an underserved urban area. When beginning the process of identifying community needs, what is the first thing the agency should do?
    a. mail a survey to local households to acquire demographic information
    b. contact and establish networks with local community leaders and ask for their input
    c. start a program immediately—before funding gets used up in research
    d. use the funding primarily for research, so future programs are better targeted

27. The Stanford Prison Experiment ended early because
    a. The "guards" were abusive.
    b. The "prisoners" were not safe.
    c. The social context of "prison" created an unsafe environment for the "prisoners" and "guards."
    d. The experimenters learned what they wanted to know faster than they'd expected.

28. Jane's husband expects her to create fabulous dinner parties for his boss, to be the perfectly available mother to their children, and to be ready for sex several nights a week. He also expects her to continue working the 12-hour shifts of a registered nurse. What problem (aside from a selfish mate) is Jane MOST likely experiencing?
    a. role complementarity
    b. role discomplementarity
    c. role ambiguity
    d. role overload

29. A teacher who allows boys to act out in class because "boys will be boys" while punishing girls who act out, is MOST likely discriminating against girls based on his concept of
    a. gender gap
    b. gender identity
    c. gender roles
    d. gender equity

30. Uneducated Caucasian men who join racist groups are NOT practicing the following concept:
    a. ethnology
    b. ethnic intimidation
    c. ethnoviolence
    d. ethnocentrism

31. Which psychodynamic construct is considered to be the basis of homophobia?
   a. homophily
   b. homoeroticism
   c. latent homosexuality
   d. the id

32. Which construct theorized by Sigmund Freud correlates to the "parent" in transactional analysis?
   a. id
   b. ego
   c. superego
   d. psyche

33. Rose often becomes frustrated in school, makes loud noises in public, and doesn't understand what people are saying to her. She often seems rude. To her trusted teacher, she fluently describes a life of loneliness and confusion, but even in her family, no one understands her. She cannot read as well as most adolescents in her age group, but her IQ is quite high. However, she is considering not going to college because she thinks it would be too difficult.
What is MOST likely Rose's problem?
   a. Rose has elective mutism.
   b. Rose has autism.
   c. Rose is hearing impaired.
   d. Rose is visually impaired.

34. Susan has to leave her study group early on Friday evenings to be home before dark. She cannot attend concerts or ball games scheduled for Saturdays. When she was 13, an important event marked her entry into adulthood. What religion is Susan most likely a member of?
   a. Islam
   b. Buddhism
   c. Hinduism
   d. Judaism

35. A man throws his half-smoked cigar out the car window. Another man picks it up, pinches the burnt end off, and puts it in his pocket. What are these men LEAST likely to have in common?
   a. education
   b. socioeconomic status
   c. occupation
   d. nicotine addiction

36. Bob grew up in an impoverished household, as did both his parents. He is often unemployed and relies on the local food bank to get enough to eat. He has no savings and lives in a rented room when he's working his seasonal job, and he lives at shelters during the rest of the year. What sort of poverty would describe Bob's life so far?
   a. relative poverty
   b. marginal poverty
   c. elective poverty
   d. residual poverty

37. What is the term for the lack of advancement of women and people of color in an organization when they possess the skills and experience to advance but are not promoted?
    a. glass ceiling
    b. fear of success
    c. fear of failure
    d. pay equity

38. A social worker has her first counseling session with a young Native American man, and she finds it nearly impossible to get him to look her in the eye, much less to talk at any level beyond answering intake questions about his age and address. She is worried that he may be schizoid, although the school counselor who referred him gave a preliminary diagnosis of an adjustment disorder. What accounts for the difference in the counselors' opinions of the young man's problem?
    a. inappropriate affect
    b. cultural confusion
    c. cultural competence
    d. discrimination

39. A recently retired middle-aged couple find themselves sharing their downsized home with their daughter, son-in-law, and two grandchildren. Although the situation is temporary, no one can predict when the younger couple will find work after losing their business to bankruptcy. The older couple find themselves stressed, and the time they had looked forward to spending in a second honeymoon is being spent with crying children and an overfilled house. They come to counseling to address their recently started, constant bickering. What is the FIRST thing their social worker should do?
    a. bring in the younger couple for family counseling
    b. provide job assistance to the younger couple
    c. help the older couple find ways to support each other and their marriage
    d. analyze the bickering and suggest alternative ways to communicate

40. What is the decision-making model that explains how policy is created from high-level business leaders influencing politicians, with no influence allowed from other levels of society?
    a. Yale polyarchy power model
    b. decision process model
    c. traditional model
    d. power pyramid model

41. What is the BEST term for meeting the expectations of success for oneself, one's family and friends, and the surrounding culture?
    a. social functioning
    b. social cost
    c. social mobility
    d. social stratification

42. An unmarried middle-aged client of Italian descent presents at a feminist therapy center with generalized anxiety and strongly conflicted feelings about her father. While she admits he "may be a little pushy," the examples she gives of her father's behavior toward her strike her counselor as being frankly domineering, sexist, and on the edge of abusive. But the client loves her father, describes him also as kind and protective of her, and is shocked when the counselor suggests that (for example) the father's recent attempt to "marry off" his daughter to a much older man is manipulative and highly inappropriate in modern-day American society. Which term MOST closely explains the behavior of the client's father?
    a. cultural bias
    b. discrimination
    c. cultural lag
    d. culture-bound syndrome

43. What is it called when a helper finds another, more positive way of looking at and describing a client's behavior or mindset, so that the client finds it a source of strength rather than a source of weakness?
    a. resiliency building
    b. positive reframing
    c. contextual therapy
    d. narrative therapy

44. In the first session with a client, what is the FIRST thing a social worker should try to establish?
    a. his or her authority as an expert
    b. the client's history
    c. client(s) feelings of trust and safety
    d. conceptualization of the client's problem

45. A client presents with persistent headaches that she attributes to stress. The intake worker asks the client questions about her general mental state, social relationships, and religious beliefs. Which of the following is the MOST important information to elicit from the client at the intake session?
    a. psychosexual history
    b. career history
    c. general medical history
    d. political beliefs

46. Which symbols are correct for male and female in the genogram?
    a. male, circle; female, triangle
    b. male, circle; female, square
    c. male, square; female, triangle
    d. male, square; female, circle

47. What is the term for obtaining additional client information from someone who is not the client—perhaps a family member, teacher, or close friend?
    a. collaborative therapy
    b. collateral information
    c. informed consent
    d. collaboration

48. Which component of a sexual history MOST helps with understanding the context of a client's inability to achieve orgasm?
    a. history of drug and alcohol use
    b. information about sexual practices
    c. length of relationships
    d. reproductive history

49. What is the name of the frequently used comprehensive family history tool that contains information across generations?
    a. the family tree
    b. genotype
    c. genogram
    d. genetic history

50. What is the BEST name for people who are simultaneously raising their children and caring for their elderly parents?
    a. generation X
    b. baby boomers
    c. sandwich generation
    d. codependents

51. What did Virginia Satir often do in her therapy sessions that therapists today are cautioned not to do?
    a. confronted her clients
    b. touched her clients
    c. analyzed her clients
    d. directed her clients

52. A family therapist tells her clients that one of the rules in her sessions is "everybody talks." She asks each person to tell her what they think the main problem is, and she notices and sometimes even comments on nonverbal communications between family members that facilitate or hinder communication. What does this method do directly for the therapist, but only indirectly for the family?
    a. formulates the problem using different perspectives
    b. involves all members and gives each permission to speak
    c. identifies family rules about who speaks and who typically gives or denies permission
    d. delineates the power structure, hierarchies, and alliances in the family

53. Salvador Minuchin's model of structural family therapy did NOT focus on which concept?
    a. enmeshment
    b. disengagement
    c. second-order change
    d. solution-focused interventions

54. In family systems and group therapy, what is "joining"?
    a. when family members or group clients feel connected and close to one another
    b. enmeshment
    c. when the therapist becomes accepted as part of the group and works from "the inside" to effect positive change
    d. when one part of the family or group bonds together to confront another faction

- 109 -

55. Which of the following is LEAST likely to be part of the process of formulating a client system's problem?
    a. using a strengths-based approach
    b. defining the problem as exactly as possible
    c. pinpointing who or what is to blame
    d. determining what the problem is not

56. In their first session, the private social worker interrupted the client's description of what brought her in, to tell her that he could solve her problem. When she stated that the man she was seeing and wanted to break up with was unusually jealous and possessive, the social worker recommended couples counseling, saying he could fix their "relationship problem" in one intensive session, which would cost $250. The client left his office within five minutes. What was the WORST mistake the social worker made?
    a. He was too eager to help.
    b. He did not listen to or accept the client's description of the problem or the change she wanted to make.
    c. He tried to turn a single client into a couples session.
    d. He mentioned the price for his intensive sessions

57. What is NOT a common occurrence in assessing the functioning of an organization?
    a. Organizations often create, manage, and report on their own functioning.
    b. Organizations tend not to identify or report their problems.
    c. Most organizations are flexible and open to change for the greater good.
    d. For changes to take effect, they must start at the top, but top-level managers/leaders have little motivation to change the status quo.

58. In assessing community functioning, who should be contacted FIRST?
    a. members of the Census Bureau
    b. university experts in community social work
    c. assessment project leaders
    d. community members

59. What problem occurs in organizations and schools that has caused people to commit both murder and suicide?
    a. lack of respect for people's needs
    b. authoritarian structure
    c. authoritative structure
    d. bullying

60. Janice and Tim refuse to acknowledge to their counselor that they have problems in their marriage, but they blame their fights on their daughter Josie. Josie's low math grades, her annoying boyfriend, and her vegetarianism are all focused on by her parents as creating the "stress" that makes her parents fight with each other. What is the professional terms for this "blame game"?
    a. denial
    b. survival bonding
    c. redirecting
    d. family projection process

61. When building a case history of a client with serious mental illness, the social worker interviews the client but finds it nearly impossible to construct a timeline of the past five years from the client's limited ability to communicate and his lack of memory. What other resources can the social worker use to understand this client's past?
    a. asking his family about his history
    b. interviewing the client using hypnosis
    c. requesting medical, hospitalization, and psychiatric records
    d. giving the client a written questionnaire

62. Which does not describe a motivational obstacle arising from within the client?
    a. abulia
    b. amotivational syndrome
    c. motivation-capacity-opportunity theory
    d. apathy

63. Whenever the man's wife blames her lack of sexual desire as being due to undergoing menopause, she avoids looking at her husband, who in turn avoids eye contact with the social worker and his wife. Although the couple seem to accept that it is menopause that has ruined their sex life, the social worker senses that the husband is experiencing guilt and that his wife is covering up for him. Their body language is not congruent with their words. What is the term for the unintentional mismatch of body language and verbal language?
    a. communication disorder
    b. lying
    c. communication leakage
    d. collusion

64. When assessing obstacles or challenges in a client's situation, how can the social worker BEST set the stage for helping the client create solutions?
    a. focus exclusively on the challenges
    b. make a list of ways the client can overcome the challenges
    c. help the client identify her/his strengths and resources
    d. educate the client on problem solving

65. Jane has helped her client pinpoint his biggest problem and create a list of possible ways to address it. However, the client seems to find a problem with every intervention. When Jane suggests a relevant book, the client states that he doesn't read much. He refuses to join a group, saying he doesn't want to "meet a bunch of losers." He shoots down every possible intervention, and he even claims that, although it was his presenting problem and still causes him a great deal of suffering, there are other things he'd prefer to talk about in their sessions. What does this tell Jane about her work with this client?
    a. She has not found the right intervention and needs to try harder.
    b. The client isn't motivated to change at this time.
    c. She should refer this client to someone else.
    d. The presenting problem wasn't the "real" problem: Jane should start over.

66. What is NOT an example of a coping skill?
    a. controlling one's emotions
    b. seeking new information
    c. delaying gratification
    d. intellectualization

67. At what level of care would a social worker investigate persons at risk of abuse or neglect, address the situation, prevent further risk, and locate resources or better placements for that person?
    a. extended
    b. skilled
    c. intermediate
    d. protective

68. Sharon and Jack are forming a college therapy group, and they realize that the first five people to sign up have all been fairly extroverted women. They decide to place posters advertising the group in the computer labs of the chemistry, engineering, and mathematics departments. What are the coleaders trying to achieve?
    a. a structured group
    b. group balance
    c. group cohesiveness
    d. group harmony

69. Mark is 40 years old. He has been diagnosed with posttraumatic stress disorder (PTSD) and attention-deficit/hyperactivity disorder (ADHD). He has had several relationships with women that included violence. He comes to the agency as an involuntary client after receiving a ticket for texting while driving and having been fired from his job for watching online pornography. He admits to spending hours each day on porn sites, spending hundreds of dollars each month on them. Which would be the BEST hypothesis about Mark's youth?
    a. He had a learning disorder.
    b. He had ADHD.
    c. He was sexually abused.
    d. He was addicted to drugs or alcohol.

70. In a 12-step recovery program (such as Alcoholics Anonymous), what is the step that is taken in relation to family members and close friends?
    a. promising to quit the addictive behavior
    b. explaining to others why they are addicted
    c. apologizing and attempting to make amends
    d. asking for people close to them to attend meetings with them

71. A client who has been referred from his employer for missing work and underperforming arrives at a session with slurred speech, clumsy movements, and euphoria. What is the MOST likely reason for his behavior?
    a. substance dependence
    b. substance withdrawal
    c. substance abuse
    d. intoxication

72. What is the term for taking two drugs at the same time and experiencing more dramatic or larger effects than those drugs would create when taken alone?
    a. co-occurring dependence
    b. withdrawal
    c. additive effect
    d. overdose

73. Kelly spends a lot of time and energy dealing with her husband's drinking problem. She hides his liquor or pours it down the drain, and then she feels sorry for him and goes to the store to buy more. When he goes "cold turkey," his suffering is so extreme that she gives him a drink "just to get him over the hump." He blames her for making him want to drink, and she accepts that if she were easier to get along with, he would be able to maintain his sobriety. What is the clinical term for Kelly's attempts to help her husband, which also helps him keep drinking?
    a. codependency
    b. enabling
    c. passive aggression
    d. misplaced empathy

74. Which of the following is NOT considered a consumptive addiction?
    a. sex
    b. food
    c. alcohol
    d. cocaine

75. Which disorder MOST frequently occurs in association with addictive disorders, with approximately 30% of people with addictions also experiencing this problem?
    a. bipolar disorder
    b. anxiety
    c. depression
    d. obsessive-compulsive disorder (OCD)

76. What is NOT an expression of social phobia?
    a. fear of being humiliated by others
    b. intense depression
    c. intense anxiety
    d. terror of public speaking or eating in restaurants

77. What do the following disorders all have in common: amok, latah, pibloktoq, and koro?
    a. They are all physiologically based.
    b. They all involve violence.
    c. They are all culture-bound.
    d. They are all adjustment disorders.

78. Which statement about victims of sexual abuse is most likely to be true?
    a. Sexually abused children most often do not become perpetrators as adults.
    b. Perpetrators of sexual abuse were abused themselves as children.
    c. Both a and b are true.
    d. Neither a nor b is true.

79. Which of the following are signs of battered spouse syndrome?
    a. getting help, running away, and starting a new life
    b. getting an education or a job as part of a plan to become independent of the batterer
    c. being afraid to leave, not trusting one's instincts, not getting help, becoming violent
    d. being indecisive but acting unafraid and standing up to the battering spouse

80. Which is not usually a cause of PTSD?
    a. accident
    b. war
    c. marital problems
    d. disasters

81. An 18-year-old client presents with an aloof manner that is indifferent and withdrawn. He has no friends and spends most of his time outside of school building model airplanes. He does not fit the criteria for autism disorders. His mother tells the social worker that he's always been "different; impossible to talk to; not a bad boy, just not really there, somehow." What is the most likely DSM-5 diagnosis for this young man?
    a. schizoid disorder of adolescence
    b. schizophreniform disorder
    c. schizoid personality disorder
    d. highly introverted personality

82. Which of the following is NOT considered a neurobiological disorder?
    a. anorexia nervosa
    b. schizophrenia
    c. bipolar disorder
    d. major depression

83. What is "cluttering"?
    a. an obsessive-compulsive disorder that causes people to become unable to get rid of objects in their homes
    b. frequent repetitions of words or parts of words, disrupted speech that worsens when the person is under pressure
    c. speech that is so fast and erratic that others find it difficult to understand
    d. untidy but otherwise normal housekeeping

84. A 70-year-old man is referred to a social worker for confusion, emotionality, and unusual lethargy. In the session, he mentions having headaches and needing help organizing his daily schedule of medications. What is the FIRST thing the social worker should do for this client before working with him in therapy?
    a. Have him assessed for Alzheimer's disease.
    b. Assess his reality orientation.
    c. Help him schedule an appointment for a review of his medications.
    d. Ask if he is depressed.

85. Which is LEAST likely to be associated with a history of childhood sexual abuse?
    a. sexual pain disorders
    b. post-traumatic stress disorder
    c. fibromyalgia
    d. addictive behaviors

86. Which behavior is NOT considered one of emotional abuse and neglect?
    a. clearly favoring other family members
    b. belittling
    c. blaming
    d. enabling

87. Which outcome of physical neglect is MOST likely to be fatal if caught too late?
    a. shaken baby syndrome
    b. nonorganic failure to thrive
    c. deprivational dwarfism
    d. neuromotor handicaps

88. In which stage of domestic violence or intimate partner abuse do the daily stresses of life prompt verbal abuse, with the abused person trying, without success, to placate the abuser?
    a. acute battering
    b. honeymoon
    c. tension building
    d. apologizing

89. A behavioral pattern of passivity, exhibited by victims of abuse and other forms of exploitation, where inaction stems from the belief that there is no way to get help is called
    a. self-defeating personality disorder
    b. masochism
    c. learned helplessness
    d. apathy

90. According to current statistics from the National Coalition Against Domestic Violence (NCADV), how many women and men experience physical abuse by an intimate partner per year?
    a. 50,000
    b. 5,000,000
    c. 7,500,000
    d. 10,000,000

91. What is the LEAST likely to be an outcome of emotional, physical, or sexual abuse?
    a. low self-esteem
    b. eating disorders
    c. difficulty forming healthy relationships
    d. anxiety and depression

92. What is the MOST current term for someone who becomes a resident in another country without going through lawful channels?
    a. undocumented alien
    b. illegal alien
    c. illegal immigrant
    d. foreigner

93. Which is NOT one of the features of an existential life review?
    a. It helps people overcome loneliness.
    b. It helps people find meaning in their past.
    c. It helps people face and resolve unresolved conflicts.
    d. It helps people face dying.

94. What does existentialist therapist Irvin Yalom NOT list as part of the human condition?
    a. isolation
    b. meaninglessness
    c. mortality
    d. imprisonment

95. The stages of grief as theorized by Elizabeth K?bler-Ross include denial, anger, bargaining, depression, and acceptance. What is an important fact that she discussed after publication of her work and that many practitioners are not aware of?
    a. The listed stages are not relevant to people undergoing any loss but bereavement.
    b. The stages can only be passed through in the order listed above.
    c. The stages are not necessarily passed through in order, and they may even be revisited.
    d. The stages do not apply to people facing their own death.

96. Maria is raising her two children alone, working full time, and caring for her mother, who has recently started wandering away from the house and becoming lost. Maria has started experiencing bouts of anger, followed by apathy. She feels she has more responsibility than she can handle and that she has little control over the financial and physical safety of her family. She continues being a responsible employee and a nurturing caregiver, but she is feeling the pressure. What is the most correct term for Maria's problem?
    a. existential crisis
    b. identity crisis
    c. burnout
    d. generalized anxiety

97. Which is the strongest predictor of a suicide attempt?
    a. threatening to commit suicide
    b. hopelessness
    c. obtaining the means to commit suicide or making a plan
    d. a history of suicide attempts

98. What is NOT a component of shared responsibility in mental health crisis treatment, according to the Substance Abuse and Mental Health Services Administration (SAMHSA)?
    a. helping the individual in crisis regain control
    b. considering the individual in crisis to be an active participant rather than a passive recipient of services
    c. allotting complete control to the helping agency
    d. establishing feelings of personal safety for the person in crisis

99. In situations of domestic violence, what increases the incidence of murder by 500%?
    a. if the victim fights back
    b. if the abuser has a history of substance abuse
    c. if sexual jealousy is involved
    d. if there is a gun in the house

100. The treatment plan concludes with the statement that the client will feel better about herself by the end of treatment. What is wrong with the statement of this goal?
    a. It is too modest and not worth the time in therapy.
    b. It can't be subjectively assessed.
    c. It can't be objectively proven.
    d. It is too vague as to the time period involved, and the outcome can't be measured.

101. A new client is outwardly passive about her problem and seems to be waiting for the social worker to "make something happen." What is the BEST course of action for the social worker?
    a. Actively guide the client in addressing the problem, until the client becomes more intrinsically motivated.
    b. Rather than making something happen, explore with the client her building frustration over wanting something from the therapist and not getting it.
    c. Encourage the client to talk about her feelings and try to address her lack of participation without blaming her.
    d. Refer the client to a group focusing on decision-making skills.

102. How can a social worker best begin work with a client so that both parties have clear expectations of the goals, the time period the work will cover, and each one's responsibilities in the working relationship?
    a. by having an implicit understanding naturally arise during the work
    b. by discussing and even writing goals, processes, and timetables at the beginning of the counseling work and reevaluating priorities at regular intervals
    c. by discussing goals, processes, and timetables as the work proceeds
    d. by reviewing together what's been achieved at the end of treatment

103. What is it called when, as termination approaches, the client's symptoms, which have been addressed and ameliorated, return, seemingly in full force?
    a. working through
    b. flight from health
    c. flight into illness
    d. resistance

104. In intervening in a crisis, which step will the social worker take FIRST?
    a. identifying the impact of the problem on the client system
    b. helping the client learn new and better ways of coping
    c. helping the client experience growth and change
    d. acknowledging the problem with the client

105. In cognitive behavioral therapy, what is NOT part of thought switching?
    a. saying "stop" to negative thoughts
    b. distracting oneself from rumination
    c. practicing relaxation
    d. substituting positive thoughts for negative ones

106. Although Sophie doesn't ignore the fact that her client has a gambling addiction and bipolar personality disorder, in sessions, she focuses on his skill at calculating statistics and his love of animals. Which perspective is Sophie operating from with this client?
    a. a strengths-based perspective
    b. a solution-focused perspective
    c. a structural perspective
    d. a behavioral perspective

107. Which is NOT part of problem-solving casework?
    a. open-ended, client-centered (fairly unlimited) timelines
    b. clearly defined goals
    c. focused interventions
    d. attention to the environmental aspects of the client's situation

108. In which technique of skills teaching are clients the LEAST active?
    a. role playing
    b. didactic teaching
    c. empty chair
    d. family sculpting

109. Which is NOT an outcome rating for the person-in-environment (PIE) system?
    a. severity index
    b. duration index
    c. coping index
    d. crisis index

110. In which model are the following concepts used: active listening, "I" messages, no-lose conflict resolution, behavior window?
    a. transactional analysis
    b. tough-love parenting
    c. parent effectiveness training (PET)
    d. rational emotive therapy

111. Kay is leading a group focused on expressing their feelings and needs and standing up for their rights and beliefs. Which coping skill is being addressed MOST especially in the group?
    a. assertiveness
    b. positive thinking
    c. healthy communication
    d. stress reduction

112. In anger management training, which technique includes getting a different perspective on the situation?
    a. relaxation
    b. communication
    c. cognition
    d. environmental change

113. In effective group therapy, where does positive change primarily originate from?
    a. from the group leader's decisions on behalf of the group
    b. from powerful or charismatic members of the group who take the lead
    c. from the process of the group itself
    d. from the group leader managing the group unobtrusively and with respect

114. At which stage of community-based decision making do members of the community justify the correctness of the decision(s) they've made?
    a. orientation
    b. conflict
    c. emergence
    d. reinforcement

115. Which piece of federal legislation gives individuals access to their medical records as well as control over the disclosure and use of their health information?
    a. the Patient Protection and Affordable Care Act (ACA) of 2010
    b. the Patient Self-Determination Act (PSDA) of 1991
    c. the Health Insurance Portability and Accountability Act (HIPAA) of 1996
    d. the Americans with Disabilities Act (ADA) of 1990

116. At which level of intervention would social workers act to bring about change in state adoption laws?
    a. micro
    b. mezzo
    c. macro
    d. meso

117. Which type of organizational theory has been criticized for explaining the motivation to work as solely dependent on financial reward?
    a. systems approach
    b. human relations theory
    c. sociotechnical approach
    d. scientific management theory

118. An agency has received a government contract to help 175 Syrian refugees settle into the community as quickly as possible. Because most of them do not speak English, timely and cost-effective interventions are being considered. Which would be the MOST helpful intervention?
    a. 1:1 ESL tutoring with trained volunteers
    b. ESL classes in small groups of 6–8 people
    c. ESL classes in larger groups of 10–20 people
    d. online self-study options in ESL

119. Which type of mezzo-level social work interventions creates jobs and housing, cleans up area neighborhoods, and improves local education resources?
    a. building resiliency
    b. organizing
    c. building capacity
    d. planning

120. A complete intervention consists of
    a. researching behavior, development, risk, and resilience
    b. identifying and teaching skills, techniques, and strategies aimed to increase well-being
    c. conducting reviews during the intervention, at termination, and after termination
    d. identifying clients' needs, abilities, and circumstances as well as all of the above

121. Which DSM-5 resource helps social workers clarify the impact of culture on clients' symptoms and possible treatment options?
    a. the list of culture-bound syndromes
    b. the cultural assimilation interview
    c. the cultural formulation interview guide
    d. the assessment of cultural deprivation

122. Which one of these four case management activities is most likely to prevent clients from "falling through the cracks" of multiple services?
    a. planning
    b. linking/linkage
    c. monitoring
    d. advocacy

123. Liz has screened several people by phone. She has helped one client acquire his military service record for required documentation, reviewed guidelines and explained benefits and services to him, and completed an application on his behalf. What is her overall purpose in these activities?
    a. matching client needs to services
    b. referring the client to a different agency
    c. following up an intervention
    d. determining the client's eligibility for services

124. Which physical system includes glands and hormones?
    a. lymphatic
    b. immune
    c. endocrine
    d. urinary

125. What is one potential problem with an intradisciplinary team approach?
    a. People share the same professional values.
    b. Supervision and mentoring may be provided.
    c. Perspectives may be too similar to create new solutions to problems.
    d. Services may be fragmented.

126. Which is NOT a rule for correct case recording?
    a. It should contain a clear, unbiased statement of facts.
    b. It should be free of objective comment.
    c. All decisions should be documented.
    d. It should be updated in a timely manner.

127. For additional protection of client confidentiality, what is the BEST location for psychotherapy notes?
   a. with the intake information
   b. with the service plan and goals
   c. with the consent forms and releases
   d. in a secure place outside of the client files

128. Which is the MOST important potentially negative outcome of a poorly written or incorrect case report to external organizations?
   a. Social workers and services will lose credibility.
   b. Opportunities for clients may be limited by lack of information.
   c. Reports will be less useful to the external organization.
   d. Irrelevant or inappropriate information could cause harm to clients.

129. Which of the following is NOT true regarding consent for the release of information?
   a. Clients should be given a copy of their signed release form.
   b. Third-party requests need separate consent forms.
   c. Clients cannot revoke consent once they have signed a form.
   d. The time period during which disclosure is approved should be included on the form.

130. Which helping behavior will NOT further the therapeutic working alliance?
   a. sympathetic comments
   b. communicating understanding in a helpful way
   c. being genuine
   d. using positive regard

131. When the client lowers her voice, clasps her hands, and leans forward, the social worker also leans forward and drops his voice. What is this nonverbal communication technique called?
   a. mirroring or mimesis
   b. empathic communication
   c. reflecting
   d. validating

132. Louise began therapy with a presenting problem of experiencing increasing anxiety and panic attacks when driving alone or riding in the car with her husband. As the social worker took her history, she also learned that Louise has been having marital problems and is considering leaving her husband, but is terrified of being alone again. When Louise casually mentions that she doesn't feel anxious when riding with her friends as a passenger, her social worker intuits that the marriage trouble and the driving phobia are related, and that the client's panic is arising from her feelings about her marriage. Which type of content has brought the therapist to this hypothesis about her client's presenting problem?
   a. neurotic symptoms
   b. overt content
   c. manifest content
   d. latent content

133. What is the technique called when a social worker restates the client's message in different words, to make sure the social worker's understanding is correct?
   a. normalization
   b. clarification
   c. interpretation
   d. reframing

134. Which technique can "shut down" client communication if used at the wrong time in the therapeutic relationship?
   a. asking open-ended questions
   b. taking a nonjudgmental stance
   c. confrontation
   d. interruption

135. Which is the MOST helpful technique to use with clients in a highly emotional state?
   a. using logic
   b. using silence
   c. offering advice
   d. making small talk

136. Why does single-subject research possess inherently poor external validity?
   a. Establishing good external validity requires a large number of participants.
   b. Establishing good external validity requires a small number of participants.
   c. Strong external validity means that the treatment caused the outcome.
   d. When internal validity is good, external validity is poor.

137. What assessment uses a Likert-type scale for clients to report their therapeutic outcomes?
   a. progress scaling
   b. outcome scaling
   c. task-attainment scaling
   d. goal-attainment scaling

138. What is it called when a social worker takes unfair advantage of a professional relationship to advance her standing financially?
   a. dual relationship
   b. retirement planning
   c. manipulation
   d. conflict of interest

139. According to the National Association of Social Workers (NASW) Code of Ethics, with whom could a social worker ethically have an intimate relationship?
   a. a client's parent
   b. a former client
   c. a client's ex-spouse, if more than three years have passed
   d. another social worker

140. Barbara has learned that her new client, Jim, is also her mother's legal advisor, and he occasionally lunches with her mother to discuss business. Her mother is unaware of the counseling relationship between them. Barbara explains to Jim that there is a conflict of interest in their working together and that her main concern is making sure his interests and confidentiality remain protected. What is the BEST action Barbara can take next?
    a. Keep working with Jim, but try to be aware of potential conflicts.
    b. Refer Jim to someone else.
    c. Ask Jim to tell her mother about the counseling arrangement.
    d. Terminate the counseling relationship.

141. Which value would NOT inhibit the therapeutic relationship if held by a social worker?
    a. universalism
    b. dichotomous thinking
    c. nonjudgmental acceptance
    d. liking to have power over others

142. When must a social worker NOT terminate a client's therapy due to financial considerations?
    a. when the client is not paying an overdue balance
    b. when the client is an imminent threat to self or others
    c. when the client has been fully informed of his or her financial obligations to the agency or worker
    d. when the client has already been made aware of the consequences of nonpayment.

143. What is it called when a social worker's personal values conflict with his or her professional ones or when a social worker's values conflict with those of the agency?
    a. ethical conflict
    b. ethical code
    c. conflict of interest
    d. ethical dilemma

144. In facing an ethical conflict, what is the FIRST thing a social worker should do?
    a. speak with his or her supervisor
    b. consult with a colleague
    c. consult the DSM-5
    d. consult the NASW Code of Ethics

145. Which of the following is NOT covered in mandated reporting laws?
    a. abuse and neglect
    b. threat of harm
    c. impaired professional
    d. tax fraud

146. Which pair are NOT core values in social work?
    a. service, social justice
    b. intelligence, caring
    c. dignity and worth of the person
    d. integrity, competence

147. When should social workers discuss with clients the rights to and limits of confidentiality?
    a. once the client is comfortable with the social worker
    b. when situations arise that threaten confidentiality
    c. as soon as possible when beginning the relationship
    d. within the first month of meeting

148. A social worker has been ordered by the court to disclose information without the client's consent. She knows the disclosure of this information will harm the client. In what order should she take the following actions?
        1. ask the court to seal the file, making it unavailable to the public
        2. try to limit the scope of information, providing as little as possible
        3. ask the court to withdraw the order
        4. provide the requested information

    a. 1,2,3,4
    b. 3,2,1,4
    c. 4,2,3,1
    d. 2,4,1,3

149. What should a social worker NOT do upon receiving a subpoena?
    a. respond
    b. claim privileged information
    c. wait for a court order before acting
    d. turn over the records immediately

150. What does the NASW Code of Ethics say about client confidentiality and the media?
    a. The public has the right to know.
    b. Social workers can only disclose information that will shield the client from media scrutiny.
    c. Client confidentiality should be protected from the media.
    d. The media can be informed if they sign a nondisclosure agreement.

151. How can a social worker guarantee to individuals in family or group therapy that other group members won't disclose confidential information?
    a. by discussing it in the group and reaching a consensus
    b. It is not possible to guarantee all members will respect the rules of confidentiality.
    c. by relying on the tact of the members
    d. by a written agreement signed by everyone

152. What is MOST true about allowing clients to access their records?
    a. Social workers should never deprive clients of access.
    b. Clients should only rarely be given access.
    c. Access should only be withheld if compelling evidence shows that access to records would cause harm to the client or someone else.
    d. Clients should only have access with the social worker there to explain.

153. Besides thoroughly understanding the ethical standards in regard to releasing confidential information about minor clients to parents or guardians, what is the MOST important thing a social worker can do to protect the confidentiality of minor clients?
    a. consider the existence and requirements of any parental custody arrangements
    b. know the rights of any involved adults to access records or consent to their release
    c. know the laws about protecting and releasing minors' records
    d. know the reason for the requested information

154. When may a social worker limit a client's right to self-determination?
    a. never: the client must always have this right
    b. when the social worker knows the client is making a mistake
    c. when the client is not thinking clearly
    d. when the client's action will create serious, imminent harm for the client or others

155. What is NOT part of gaining a client's informed consent to services?
    a. promising that the services will solve his or her problems
    b. clearly explaining the risks of services
    c. clearly explaining the client's right to withdraw or refuse consent
    d. clearly explaining the limitations involved in the rights of involuntary clients to refuse services

156. Under what circumstances would a client's consent to disclosure not be required?
    a. to third-party payers
    b. when the social worker uses the information for teaching or training
    c. when consultants are involved
    d. when the social worker is defending him- or herself in a lawsuit brought by the client

157. Which is not true about working with clients who lack the capacity to make informed decisions?
    a. Clients' wishes aren't considered relevant to the process.
    b. A third party must give informed consent and the client must assent.
    c. Social workers must try to explain information to clients in ways they can understand.
    d. Social workers must take reasonable steps to protect their clients.

158. Where are the laws to be found that regulate the emancipation of minors?
    a. the Bill of Rights
    b. federal legislation
    c. states' legislation
    d. county bylaws

159. What is the primary goal in permanency planning?
    a. to enrich the home life of the child
    b. to assure the child's safety in the home
    c. to get children back into their original homes
    d. to provide caregivers with support services

160. Fran isn't sure that her client Lisa can continue to live independently because Lisa has had several strokes that have affected her ability to be independent in activities of daily living. How can Fran make a determination that will also provide the documentation necessary to help Lisa be considered for additional household assistance?

    a. Fran should ask Lisa if she can remain independent.
    b. Fran should use the World Health Organization's Disability Assessment Schedule (WHODAS) to calculate the extent of Lisa's capabilities.
    c. Fran should consult with Lisa's doctor.
    d. Fran should assume that Lisa is all right unless something happens that indicates otherwise.

161. In which case would a social worker determine that a client is not competent to provide consent?

    a. The client is illiterate.
    b. The client cannot cook for himself.
    c. The client is extremely aged.
    d. Legal proceedings have pronounced the client to be incompetent.

162. What is the central concept in social work, and one the social worker is obliged to respect and protect for clients?

    a. self-esteem
    b. self-determination
    c. informed consent
    d. confidentiality

163. What supersedes the social worker's commitment to respecting clients' decisions?

    a. legal obligations and the responsibility to society at large
    b. the social worker's self-determination
    c. the vulnerability of the client
    d. the importance of human relationships

164. In which therapeutic practice does the social worker defuse anger, establish rapport, and increase the client's exploration of the self and his or her problems?

    a. acceptance
    b. transference
    c. empathy
    d. countertransference

165. At which level of the psyche, according to Freudian theory, does transference operate?

    a. the conscious
    b. the unconscious
    c. the subconscious
    d. the superego

166. What, combined with accepting the client, helps the social worker bring about change?

    a. advising
    b. praising
    c. giving objective feedback
    d. giving emotional feedback

167. What may be a result of inappropriate self-disclosure by a social worker to the client?
   a. The client may realize that he or she is not alone in his or her feelings or situation.
   b. The client and social worker may begin a real friendship.
   c. The social worker may resolve issues in his or her own countertransference.
   d. Disclosure may blur or violate boundaries in the client-helper relationship.

168. What is it called when a social worker experiences upsetting symptoms related to a trauma that a client has described in therapy?
   a. burnout
   b. compassion fatigue
   c. secondary or vicarious trauma
   d. countertransference

169. Jack is trying to explain to his supervisor Bill about how his client Susan "just sits there saying nothing, making me feel stupid." Jack's frustration at Susan has taken on an overwhelming aspect, and feeling it, Bill can't think of anything to say. He just "sits there, saying nothing." Jack interprets Bill's silence as criticism: He thinks that Bill thinks he's an idiot, just like Susan does. What does this awkward situation best exemplify?
   a. poor communication
   b. transference
   c. countertransference
   d. parallel process

170. What is the most important goal in conducting professional evaluations of social workers?
   a. to satisfy the administrative requirements of the agency
   b. to identify social workers' strengths and weaknesses
   c. to improve service delivery
   d. to give supervisees suggestions for improvement

Answers and Explanations

1. B: Josie is at the teething stage, which usually takes place between the ages of 4 and 8 months.

2. D: The circumference of the head increases rapidly from birth through the first few month of life and steadily during the first years, until the child reaches 5 years of age.

3. A: Piaget's model posits the attainment of the principle of conservation between the ages of 7 and 8. Conservation is the cognitive stage at which a child understands that pouring liquid into a taller glass from a shorter one does not mean that there is now more liquid in the glass.

4. A: Spina bifida occurs when the fetus' spine does not close correctly in its early development. One cause of spina bifida is a lack of folic acid during pregnancy.

5. D: Attachment disorders (as opposed to autism spectrum disorders) are usually found in children whose caregivers' behaviors are dysfunctional. The child's seeming inability to attach is based on his or her reaction to a caregiver whose parenting skills are deficient.

6. B: Autonomy versus shame takes place between the ages of 1 and 3, the time in life when children are being toilet trained. Erikson theorized that harsh toilet training methods would create withholding or "anal-retentive" personality traits, and that permissive toilet training would lead to "anal-expressive" traits.

7. C: According to Freud, the little boy wants to possess his mother. He fears that his father, knowing of his rivalry, will castrate him. Penis envy was Freud's idea that little girls, wishing for the freedom of the masculine life, wished to become boys.

8. C: Oxytocin is known as the "love hormone." It is present during labor, breastfeeding, lovemaking, cuddling, and other bonding experiences such as playing with pets. As a drug, it has been used to precipitate labor.

9. D: The man is projecting his lack of desire for a committed relationship onto the woman. In substitution, he would be more likely to claim he wants something more exclusive because that is more socially acceptable and also something he is more likely to get from his dating partner (in layperson's terms, we'd call that "settling" for something). In reaction formation, he would take a stand opposite to what he really feels; and in rationalization, he would come up with a set of "reasonable explanations" about why a committed relationship would not be sensible.

10. C: By removing the man from his wife and removing herself from the rest of the group, the daughter is showing that, although the mother and son have a close relationship, the family as a whole has split apart.

11. B: Maslow posited that one could not reach higher levels of the hierarchy before attaining the preceding levels. Although esteem does include self-esteem and esteem by others, the stage of self-actualization is the one in which the individual is most likely to have the stability and security to engage in spiritual development.

12. C: Although Harry's mother may think that his development is abnormally slow, most children start crawling between ages 7 and 10 months, and some even skip crawling and go straight to toddling. The mother seems to be comparing her son unfavorably (and maybe unrealistically) to the children in his playgroup, hoping to use his development to bolster her egoic needs. The caseworker would do best to reassure the mother that Harry will crawl soon and to recommend patience with the natural process of his growth.

13. C: Adolescence is noted for being a time when people experiment with clothing, lifestyle, challenging boundaries, drugs and alcohol—nearly anything that coincides with the all-important life task of differentiating from one's parent and becoming an individual.

14. C: People who have children younger in life tend to attain less education, which compromises their employability and leads to a greater chance of poverty.

15. D: Generativity is the midlife ideal: The individual feels that life has a purpose and that he or she is contributing to the good of the community and the family. Work is satisfying and emotions are stable and healthy. Generativity versus stagnation occurs between the ages of 35 and 64.

16. B: Simon's age, change of personality, aggressive behavior, and confusion point to senile dementia and possibly Alzheimer's disease.

17. A: Little children who are securely attached will make sure that their primary caregiver is nearby when they encounter a new situation or person. The other three behaviors described in this item are those of reactive or disinhibited children, whose lack of attachment to a caregiver is expressed in inappropriately close or distant behaviors.

18. C: The need for food is at the first level of Maslow's hierarchy of needs, the physiological level. The five levels include the following:
1. physiological
2. safety/security
3. love and belonging
4. esteem
5. self-actualization

19. C: Competition is not considered a useful factor in building resiliency. Resiliency factors focus on achievement of an individual's life skills, fostering competency, noting strengths rather than weaknesses and maintaining a sense of optimism.

20. A: In projection, the defended person perceives their own feelings or thoughts as coming from the other person. For example, an angry person who doesn't want to "own" his anger may attribute it to his partner, saying, "Why are you always so full of rage?" In reaction formation, the defense takes the form of acting in a way opposite to what one really feels, so a person suffering from deep sadness may try to cover it up with a cheery facade. Refusal isn't a defense mechanism, but it may be confused in this case with denial, which is a refusal to accept what one knows "inside" to be true.

21. D: The concept of the inferiority complex arose from Erikson's eight-stage model of psychosocial development. In the fourth stage, between the ages of 6 and 11 (industry versus inferiority), children begin to compare themselves with others, and based on their accomplishments, they may judge themselves as being inferior. Erikson recommended that

teachers in particular be sensitive to the risks of this stage and work to promote the confidence of children in their care.

22. C: Although Jeanette is experiencing a loss of her confidence in her roles and she is feeling pressure to be a "good daughter" to her parents, this is a crisis in reaction to her current life decision, rather than being a feature of her overall life. If it were a lifelong problem, she would be said to have identity disorder, but this is likely a temporary stage that will resolve with time.

23. C: In 1977, after analyzing studies of group work, Tuckman proposed a final stage, adjourning, which would compare with the usual termination stage of individual therapy.

24. B: In working with families and groups, the worker attempts to first establish a sense of connection with each member before turning to the details of the work. Research consistently shows that clients need to feel valued for useful work to take place.

25. D: Systems theory notes that even a positive change in one family member—especially that of the identified patient—disrupts the system, so that other family members attempt to get the family member to change back. Preventing change in one family member means the rest of the family can avoid change, even when it also means certain suffering.

26. B: Including leaders of the local community is an important first step in program planning, because it's those leaders who understand the community better than any social science expert can. They may provide helpful information about previous programs' impact, failure, or success; they can also lend credibility to agency members and help establish trust in the greater community, which will positively affect participation. Modern social programmers understand that involving community members from the needs assessment to the final wrap-up shows respect for the members of the community, builds communication, and empowers them in ways that last beyond the impact of any one program.

27. C: The experimenters never expected that the students participating in the Stanford Prison Experiment would take on their roles so quickly and completely that their identities would be subsumed and the situation would become injurious. The expectations and beliefs of both "prisoners" and "guards" created an untenable experimental situation, so the experiment ended early.

28. D: Jane is attempting to fulfill the roles of wife, mother, breadwinner, and society hostess—some of the duties and time constraints of which must occasionally conflict. Although all of her assigned roles are traditionally "feminine" (even her arduous job is stereotypically "feminine") there are simply too many expectations to meet them all successfully—a condition of overload.

29. C: The teacher who has different expectations and standards for boys and girls is practicing gender bias in favor of boys, based on his belief that boys are "naturally" more aggressive than girls and should not be punished for their nature, and that girls who act out in class are behaving inappropriately for their gender and should be controlled.

30. A: Ethnology is the scientific study of races and their culture and history. Ethnocentrism is the belief in the superiority of one's own ethnic group, and racist groups do practice ethnic intimidation and violence.

31. C: Psychodynamic theory considers homophobia to be based on unconscious attraction to members of the same sex. In a sort of reaction formation, the client denies his own homosexual urges by acting fearful and angry toward homosexuals.

32. C: The superego was considered to be the part of the personality that introjects the values of the parents, driving the individual's understanding of and compliance with right and wrong, morals, and ethics.

33. C: Difficulty learning to read is a particular problem for hearing-impaired students, and many hearing-impaired people grow up in families in which other members do not learn sign language, and attend schools in which there are limited opportunities to interact with teachers and students who know how to use sign language. Frustration with not being able to communicate and with not catching verbal cues can make deaf people seem rude to others. Because Rose communicates fluently with her teacher, elective mutism and autistic disorders would be ruled out in this example.

34. D: Susan is most likely Jewish: The Jewish Sabbath begins on Friday at sundown and continues through Saturday. At the age of 13, Jewish girls and boys become adults in their faith, with a ceremony called the bat mitzvah (girls) or the bar mitzvah (boys).

35. B: One man can afford to throw a half-smoked cigar from his car; the other, traveling on foot, values it enough to pick it up for later. Whatever the educational and occupational background of the second man, it is highly unlikely that he has as many financial resources as the first man.

36. D: Residual poverty describes people whose families have been poor for many generations and who experience long-term poverty. In marginal poverty, people may sometimes earn more than the poverty level, but they return to poverty through periodic job loss and lack of skills. Relative poverty is when people are poor compared to the mainstream—so in a wealthy community, someone may be relatively poor without being absolutely poor.

37. A: In the "glass ceiling" effect, organizational inequality is not overtly stated in policy, but employees who are not white and male are disproportionately passed over for promotion at higher levels of government, industry, and academia.

38. C: The social worker has not encountered clients from this culture before and has misinterpreted the client's lack of eye contact (or tact) and unwillingness to talk about himself (which would be rude in front of a strange professional woman). What she sees as a potential mental illness is in fact considered respectful manners in the client's culture—something the school counselor, with her familiarity of that culture, understood.

39. C: The older couple is reacting to the stress of sharing their home, and they have lost their way as a couple. The first actions are to address the couple's feeling that their marriage is in trouble and to help them remember how important it is—so important that they are asked to work on their marriage rather than focusing on the rest of the family. Helping this couple reestablish their solidarity in the onslaught of family members will help them undertake the rest of the problems as a pair working together, rather than turning against each other.

40. D: The financially powerful can lobby and pressure politicians, using their wealth to impose decisions that benefit them on the rest of the population.

41. A: Social functioning is how we manage our self-expectations and the expectations of those around us as to how well we support ourselves and our families, how we live within the norms of our culture, and how we "succeed" financially and socially.

42. C: In cultural lag, people maintain the standards of their original culture, which may be inappropriate in the culture that they currently live. In this case, the father's patriarchal and domineering ways, normal to his cultural background, are accepted on one level as manifestations of his caring by his daughter, but they are also causing her distress because they limit her personal freedom.

43. B: Positive reframing is a technique that can be used in various types of therapy to help clients see their situation in a different light and act on it in ways they might not have otherwise considered.

44. C: A client's confidence in the genuineness and caring of the social worker forms the basis of any good client-counselor relationship; alternately, in the absence of trust, clients are unlikely to return for further sessions. Establishing a working alliance with the client is founded on the client feeling that the social worker is on his or her side, can be trusted to keep the client safe, and is acting authentically.

45. C: Obtaining a general medical history is an important part of the exam because it may give insight into symptoms and may help practitioners pinpoint patterns of social, psychological, and spiritual activities that can shed light on current and lifelong functioning. Furthermore, many psychological troubles have a physical concomitance, and practitioners should rule out potential physical ailments before planning psychological interventions.

46. D: Genograms also use vertical and horizontal lines to indicate relationships between family members.

47. B: Whereas collaboration and collaborative therapy involve two or more professionals working together to provide services, information obtained about the client from other people is called collateral information. Collateral information should be collected after the client has been informed and given his or her consent to the process.

48. A: Alcohol and drug use are frequently major contributors to sexual dysfunction.

49. C: The genogram is a diagram of the family history over three or more generations. It contains a graphic illustration of the relationships and gender of family members as well as historical data about events, illnesses, predispositions, substance abuse, occupations and education, socioeconomic status, current problems, and coping skills.

50. C: The sandwich generation got its name because its members are "sandwiched" between the needs of their children and those of their parents. They are generally late baby boomers, but because that term covers so many more aspects of that generation, "sandwich generation" is the more relevant term.

51. B: Satir frequently held clients' hands and patted them in her sessions. Although some therapists still use directive interventions when they think it would benefit the client system, ethical codes and professional caution tend to prevent therapists from touching their clients.

52. D: The therapist overtly helps the family formulate the problem, has each member speak, and brings covert communications into the open. She does not discuss the power issues in the family with the family members, but she can use what she observes to make further decisions about other interventions.

53. D: Solution-focused therapy tends to be brief and to the point, ignoring the complicated context of family dynamics in favor of directly tackling the presenting problems. Minuchin's model used family dynamics such as enmeshed or disengaged families and the need for not only solving one problem, but also for considering the impact of that change in the entire system. Changing the system (second-order change), he pointed out, was necessary for creating real, lasting change.

54. C: When the therapist has successfully joined the family or group, he or she becomes part of the group process. This is challenging work, because the pressure to conform to the group is a natural part of any group process, and yet that is exactly what the therapist must not do if he or she is going to change the dysfunctional group patterns.

55. C: Problems are identified considering environmental and social influences on the client, defining as precisely as possible the problem, its frequency and duration, and its effect on the client's functioning. Part of the process is also focusing on strengths; what is going well and is not part of the problem, a process that helps not only achieve focus on what needs change, but also empowers the client to act from acknowledging and accessing his or her strengths.

56. B: The social worker didn't respect the client enough to listen to what she said about wanting to end her relationship. He attempted to force unwanted couples' counseling on her because he had already decided that his job was to "save" her relationship.

57. C: Most organizations are not flexible, and creating change in procedures and in organizational culture is extremely difficult.

58. D: It's now commonly recognized that community members have important knowledge that experts cannot access without involving the community in assessment projects right from the beginning.

59. D: Bullying has become more noticed, due to terrible tragedies at schools, and communities are trying to address bullying at schools and online. Organizations are much slower to take action against bullying, as in companies that see bullying as a natural human expression in a competitive, hierarchical, and authoritarian organization. As many bullying experts point out, it is the structure and culture of individual organizations that allow bullying to flourish, and bullying should be addressed through the organization rather than only focusing on the individual.

60. D: In this classic scapegoating process, the married couple attempt to avoid the more frightening recognition of the problems between them by focusing the attention on their daughter and blaming her. In some families, this projection continues until the child grows up and leaves home, leaving the couple with no one to project their problem on, at which time the relationship enters a crisis.

61. C: The client does not presently have the capacity to recall or communicate details of his past, which would make a written questionnaire ineffective. Interviewing under hypnosis would likely be contraindicated for someone with serious mental illness and would probably not elicit the sought-for information. Family members might be helpful, but for obtaining facts about dates, assessments,

treatments, and outcomes, the social worker would do best to request medical and psychiatric records.

62. C: Whereas the other three terms are designated as lack of motivation within the client, the theory of motivation-capacity-opportunity tends to view clients as willing to participate as long as the intervention is appropriate and as long as no external obstacles prevent the client from taking part in the process.

63. C: Communication leakage refers to a situation in which the overt message is undermined by nonverbal cues that undermine or oppose the message.

64. C: Focusing on clients' strengths and available resources encourages problem solving and helps build hope and resiliency. Working with the client to identify strengths not only helps address the current challenges, it also teaches the client helpful life skills that can be used when facing future problems.

65. B: This is not an unusual situation: Even clients whose problems are wrecking their lives find it extremely difficult to change. In therapy, they may be labeled as "resistant" and "dumped," or conscientious helpers may struggle to suggest different solutions, only to find that nothing works—and to feel like they're failing the client. In this case, the social worker has done all she can and is working harder than her client (this is always a clue that something isn't right). She doesn't need to refer the client: He would probably act the same way with any helper. Jane's challenge is to stick with the client, to stop presenting him with solutions, and to wait until his problem becomes his problem again, not hers. If he is not motivated to change because his problem isn't causing him much suffering, he will drop out of therapy on his own. If the pressure on him has relaxed because he has shifted his responsibility for solving the problem to Jane, her relaxing of the hold on his problem will allow the pressure to rest on him again, which will eventually increase his motivation to change.

66. D: Although intellectualizing is one way people attempt to cope with challenges, it is a defense mechanism rather than a coping skill. Coping skills are positive strategies that help people manage difficulty in healthy ways.

67. D: The protective level of care is that level required for children, the elderly, people with mental retardation, and people with disabilities. "Skilled" or "extended" care is usually associated with Medicaid designations for long-term nursing facilities. Intermediate care is a designation used for older people who cannot live alone but can manage activities of daily living and are not in need of full-time nursing care.

68. B: The coleaders are trying to recruit "typical" students from the sciences—usually introverted, usually male—to balance out the outgoing female members. Whereas some groups are structured to meet the needs of a particular population (as in a group working on excessive shyness, in which everyone would be socially uncomfortable to some extent), others are built upon the idea that differences between members will enrich the experience for everyone. In such a group, leaders will seek variety in the group's members.

69. C: Mark's history of violence in his intimate relationships and his current addictions to pornography and the internet, combined with his having PTSD and ADHD, produce a constellation of conditions that points to his having been abused as a child. He may well have been addicted to drugs or alcohol at an early age because it's not uncommon for abused children to turn to drugs to

attempt to numb the pain and ease the memories of abuse, and current abuse or symptoms of PTSD will look like ADHD or learning disorders in the school setting. However, there is no current indication of drug or alcohol abuse.

70. C: Part of the 12-step process of taking responsibility for one's actions involves apologizing to those you've wronged and doing whatever you can to make things right.

71. D: Although the client may indeed be experiencing substance dependence and abusing drugs or alcohol, his behavior in the session indicates that he is currently intoxicated.

72. C: Because the substances are interacting, their effects are adding to the effects on the user.

73. B: Enabling behavior helps create situations in which the other person's dysfunction can continue. Enabling may take the form of providing the substance, but it may also happen when someone tries to deprive the addicted person of the substance, which gives that person cause for resentment and another "reason" to continue the destructive pattern.

74. A: Addictions are divided into two categories: behavioral and consumptive. Consumptive addictions are those in which the addicted person introduces a substance into his or her body, and behavioral addictions have to do with activities.

75. C: Depression is strongly associated with addiction, and in many cases, it's difficult to discern which comes first. Some theories of addiction say that people become addicted in an attempt to self-medicate their long-standing and pervasive depression.

76. B: Social phobia is an anxiety disorder, not a depressive one. Sufferers are certain other people are noticing them and laughing at them, and their anxiety becomes a vicious cycle because they're so uncomfortable in public that they do draw attention to themselves, which increases their anxiety.

77. C: Each one of these disorders is associated with a particular cultural background, and they are not recognizable in other cultures.

78. C: Although most perpetrators of sexual abuse were abused themselves as children, the majority of people who were sexually abused as children do not grow up to be perpetrators.

79. C: In battered spouse syndrome, the victim is trapped by fear and helplessness, unable to seek help or take positive action to help him- or herself. Occasionally, the near-constant terror of the victim may give way to feelings of such desperation that the victim may temporarily overcome his or her fear of being hurt again and take action with violence.

80. C: Post-traumatic stress disorder is considered to be caused by events that are not part of normal life, for example, events that are violent and/or horrifying. Unless the relationship is abusive, marital problems are, unfortunately, an all-too-usual part of life.

81. C: Because this young man's withdrawn behavior has been persistent throughout his lifespan, he would most likely be considered to have a schizoid personality. (Because he is at the age dividing adolescence from adulthood in the diagnostic criterion, without evidence that his behavior has been lifelong, he might have been diagnosed with schizoid disorder of adolescence.) Schizophreniform

disorder is much less adaptive and contains features of schizophrenia, and although someone might be considered to have a highly introverted personality, introversion is not a diagnosable condition.

82. A: Anorexia has been associated with cultural pressures that result in body image distortions and attempts to control perceived weight gain. Although it certainly has neurobiological concomitance, its cause has not been identified as organic.

83. C: In cluttering, the person's speech is "cluttered" by too many words and an uneven cadence, so that listeners can't understand the person. It differs from stuttering/stammering in that it may be partly caused by the speaker's not being sure of what he or she wants to express. In stuttering, the speaker knows what he or she wants to say, but can't say it.

84. C: Many of the elderly are overmedicated or are taking medications whose interaction effects create additional ailments, such as headaches, confusion, and emotional problems. In a medication review, each medication is considered in relation to the others, and a review may discover that medications from different doctors or for different illnesses are causing new problems for the client.

85. C: Fibromyalgia is a little-understood condition involving generalized pain and fatigue, but it is not usually associated with childhood sexual abuse.

86. D: Although enabling is a dysfunctional and harmful set of behaviors that may accompany emotional abuse or neglect, it is not particularly associated with emotional abuse, and it may be present in relationships in which the other person believes they are really caring for the other.

87. B: Although the other three conditions can be fatal, nonorganic failure to thrive is associated with neglect, not necessarily physical abuse. It is the only one of the listed conditions that can be reversed if it is caught soon enough. An important indication of physical neglect as the cause of nonorganic failure to thrive is that once babies are admitted to the hospital or placed in someone else's care, they gain weight and begin to grow.

88. C: In this stage, the physical abuse has temporarily ceased and the couple has been in the "honeymoon" period, during which the abuser has tried to make amends, has apologized, and has said that the abuse will never happen again. In the tension-building stage, which follows the honeymoon stage, the pressure again builds up, leading again to the acute battering stage.

89. C: Learned helplessness is the result of one's "learning" that obtaining help is impossible, so that the lack of help-seeking behavior may generalize to situations where help is possible, but it remains unasked-for. Learned helplessness may be one feature of self-defeating personality disorder, but additional criteria need to be met before reaching that diagnosis. Masochism implies a sexual element, which is not present in this description. Apathy, although likely a component of learned helplessness, can be found in other disorders such as depression and autism-spectrum disorders.

90. D: The NCADV estimates that 10 million people a year are physically abused by an intimate partner.

91. B: A history of abuse generates myriad physical and psychological problems, but of the group listed here, eating disorders are the least likely to occur.

92. A: Although "illegal alien" and "illegal immigrant" have been commonly used phrases more recently in use, "foreigner" is generally considered to have hostile connotations and doesn't specifically refer to one's immigration status. The current term deemed most respectful as well as descriptive is "undocumented alien."

93. A: An existential life review is often something people do informally, as they are growing old, but it can also be done with help from a social worker or other therapist as part of the dying process. Loneliness is a factor in existential work, but it is not a specific focus of the life review process.

94. D: The fourth human condition listed by Yalom is freedom. Although existentialism acknowledges the negative aspects of human life, it also focuses on our freedom to choose how we react to those negative aspects.

95. C: After her work became famous, K?bler-Ross was dismayed that practitioners and lay readers conceptualized the stages in a linear fashion, when in fact, the grief process can involve cycling back to earlier stages over longer periods of time.

96. C: Burnout is characterized by feeling that one has more responsibility than control (note that there is no change in Maria's outward behavior: She is not in crisis and is not presenting with symptoms of unusual anxiety).

97. D: Having attempted suicide before is the strongest factor is another attempt, although all the items on this list are considered important indicators of suicidality.

98. C: The treatment model of SAMHSA is client-centered and recommends that the agency exercise only as much authority over the client as is consistent with keeping the client and others safe from harm.

99. D: Guns greatly increase the potential of murder in domestic violence.

100. D: Goals should be clearly defined as to time (number of sessions, weeks, or months) and measurable indications of the outcome (post-test scores, countable behaviors, analyzable client feedback, etc.).

101. B: When someone else becomes actively involved in trying to solve the client's problem, the result will confirm the client's unexpressed belief that she lacks the competence to do it herself. The client will also be highly likely to prevent the efforts of the social worker from coming to fruition, so the social worker will experience the frustration of feeling incompetent. Rather than experiencing the countertransferential feelings of being unable to succeed, the social worker can refuse to "help" the client by not acting to solve the stated problem and instead help the client focus on the underlying issue of her lack of confidence in her abilities and the conflict around wanting someone else to take control and wishing one could succeed in controlling one's own life.

102. B: The more clearly that goals are defined, the more likely they are to be attained. Likewise, clear-cut agreements about timetables, payment, rights, and responsibilities set the stage for a transparent therapeutic alliance.

103. C: Flight into illness is a normal occurrence toward the end of therapy because the client resists the idea of once again facing the world without the therapist. The event is usually addressed

by helping the client review the progress made and his or her new coping skills learned through counseling and by the fact that the social worker will be available should the client experience new challenges. Celebrating the client's resiliency and growth helps the client end counseling with a sense of ongoing support and self-confidence.

104. D: Acknowledging the problem takes place first, enabling the client and social worker to define it as fully as possible and identify ways of addressing it.

105. B: Although distraction is sometimes used as a technique, it is not part of the process of thought switching. Typically, one recognizes that there is a negative thought and says "stop" to it, takes a moment to regroup and relax (negative thoughts generate tension and anxiety, and they make it difficult to think clearly), and, finally, substitutes a positive thought for the original one.

106. A: Sophie is focusing on her client's strengths, which has been shown to empower clients and build resiliency.

107. A: In problem-solving casework, timelines are also clearly defined, set out at the beginning of counseling, and adhered to as much as possible. Some therapists believe that by setting time limits on sessions, clients are motivated to change more quickly.

108. B: Role playing, family sculpting, and the empty chair technique are highly participatory methods; didactic teaching is what we usually think of as the "traditional" form of classroom learning, with one person dispensing information and others receiving it. It is not generally experiential, but it is based more on listening, understanding, and memorizing the information.

109. D: The severity index in the PIE system most closely identifies situations of crisis; its score indicates to what extent social work intervention is needed.

110. C: Although each of the models above may use active listening and "I" messages, no-lose conflict resolution and the idea of the behavior window, which asks clients to recognize who "owns" a particular problem, are also particular to PET.

111. A: Standing up for oneself and one's rights are key components of assertiveness training.

112. C: Changing one's perspective is a skill used in cognitive interventions, which teach clients new ways of thinking about problems and solutions. Notice that the other three options either assume the presence of another person (communication) or a mind-body approach, as in relaxation responses or environmental change.

113. C: Although the group leader(s) have responsibility for setting rules and limits and stepping in when the group is losing focus or becoming unsafe, group theory is based on the idea that in a safe environment, the work of the group creates lasting change. Theorists such as Irvin Yalom have written about group work as a near-mystical process, in which the interaction of group members and the process achieve a powerful and useful therapeutic synergy through "ordinary" group work.

114. D: In this final step of decision making, people seek information or support of their choice.

115. C: This legislation allows patients some privacy protection at the federal level, although some states have laws that supersede it by improving on it. The HIPAA privacy rule went into effect in 2003.

116. C: Working to change laws, regulations, policy, and procedures at levels larger than the smaller community (such as a neighborhood) is considered macro intervention.

117. D: Scientific management theory is one of a group of classic theories that did not take into account other factors in people's motivation to work beside those of financial gain. Other classic organizational theories include Weber's bureaucratic theory and administrative theory.

118. B: Small groups would maximize the teaching while keeping the group small enough to address other issues such as those that might arise when ESL students have also undergone the considerably traumatic experience of losing their homes, possibly experiencing violence and deprivation, and settling in a foreign culture. Training ESL tutors to also provide emotional support would be time-consuming and expensive, as well as requiring someone to oversee the tutors. Larger classes would make it difficult for teachers to maintain awareness of students' individual needs. Online study would not meet the social and acculturation needs of students and would not provide them with direct contact and support with others from their culture.

119. C: Building capacity refers to the process by which social work attempts to enhance the quality of clients' lives. Improving the environment and access to decent jobs, housing, and education are components of capacity building. Resiliency is built through identifying and maximizing client and community strengths; planning is a necessary a part of any change process; organizing uses grassroots political processes to empower people.

120. D: Interventions may look simple, but their effectiveness rests on a large number of individual processes, from initial needs assessment to post-termination evaluation.

121. C: The guide assists social workers in coming to an understanding of how the client's culture impacts his or her experience and current feelings and functioning. Such an interview should help social workers increase their cultural awareness and identify a change incident of cultural bias, as well as letting clients know that their heritage matters and is not being ignored or denigrated.

122. B: In case management, linkage or linking is the process social workers use to coordinate services, creating collaboration between different agencies, groups, or service providers on behalf of clients. The five case management activities are assessment, planning, linking, monitoring, and advocacy.

123. D: Liz is determining whether a client can participate in a program that has eligibility requirements by first identifying clients who seem to fit those requirements, helping them show that they fit (in this case by using his military records), making sure the client understands and wants to participate, and finally by completing the application for services.

124. C: In the endocrine system, glands produce and control hormones, which control growth, sexual development, and metabolism.

125. C: The argument for an interdisciplinary team approach is that professionals from different backgrounds will have different perspectives, and they will be able to generate a richer, more diverse set of constructs than a team made up of members of the same profession.

126. B: Case recording should be free of subjective comment (opinions, unverifiable statements, etc.). Objective comment is data-driven and as factual as possible.

127. D: Keeping therapy notes separated from other client files is the standard way of protecting client confidentiality.

128. D: The most important consideration is in preventing harm to the client. Paperwork, in some cases, can literally save lives or ruin them. Disclosing the wrong information, or the right information to the wrong people or at the wrong time can put clients in danger, or it can fail to remove them from a dangerous situation. Writing clearly is an important service in the protection of clients.

129. C: Clients have the right to revoke their consent, except in situations in which someone is in danger of being harmed or is being harmed.

130. A: Sympathy is not considered a helpful behavior because it comes from a place of pity. Pity differs from compassion in that it places the sympathizer above rather than being equal to the other person.

131. A: Mirroring is an effective way of connecting with others if it is done naturally, authentically, and for the right reasons. It does demonstrate empathy and shows that the listener is "really there." Reflecting and validating are verbal techniques that help the social worker clarify his or her understanding of the client's meaning (reflecting) and support the client in expressing emotional content (validating).

132. D: The underlying story of this client is that the client is conflicted about leaving her husband. The client doesn't consciously connect that conflict with her car-related phobia, but the social worker notes that anxiety and panic attacks do not happen with other people. In this case, the latent content of the client's story may be that driving is a metaphor for her life.

133. B: The social worker is clarifying his or her understanding of the client's message. In normalization, the response would be to accept the client's view as something most people would experience; in interpretation, the social worker takes the client's message one step further in drawing additional meanings from it; reframing occurs when a thought or behavior is considered from a different, more positive perspective.

134. C: Open-ended questions and a nonjudgmental stance are constants in a healthy working relationship. There is no really good time for using interruption as a technique. Confrontation, however, can be a powerful and positive intervention when used correctly and at the right time. Generally speaking, early in the establishment of the working alliance, confrontation would not be used until sufficient trust and confidence are established.

135. B: Silence can help clients calm down; it can project a feeling of care without requiring a response; it can model a more peaceable stance. When someone is caught up in negative emotions, logic, advice, and small talk are not helpful, but using silence judiciously can give the client a sense of safety and security that can help the turmoil subside.

136. A: External validity asks, "can we generalize this finding to the population at large?" To be able to state that a treatment will be successful for most people in a population, the study needs to have a sizable number of subjects in it (100 is usually considered a minimally good sample size). In single-subject research, the uniqueness of the individual can be a large factor influencing results, rather than the treatment: It's not really possible to generalize the results to the population.

137. D: In goal-attainment scaling, clients can rate their success in reaching their therapeutic goals by choosing numbers along a continuum for each item. Items are totaled based on the factors they represent within the assessment, and numbers totaled give a score that tells of the perceived effectiveness of the intervention.

138. D: When the helping relationship is used by the helper to attain personal goals, it is a conflict of interest and a violation of the ethical code.

139. D: Social workers may not have personal relationships with family members or ex-family members of clients, and they may not have sexual relationships with former clients. They also may not see their former partners as clients. But there are no restrictions on having intimate relationships with other social workers, keeping in mind that there must not be a conflict of interest (such as there would be in a manager-employee or supervisor-supervisee relationship, for example).

140. B: In this case, where Jim advises her mother on finances, which may affect her as well, it's a reasonable, sensible, and ethical decision to refer Jim to another social worker.

141. C: The other attitudes are harmful to clients, who would not be able to trust someone who thinks their way is the right way, who thinks in black and white, or who likes to feel they have the upper hand in their interactions with clients. Nonjudgmental acceptance is what all good social workers strive for.

142. B: The social worker has an ethical obligation to help the client become stabilized before pursuing nonpayment if there is danger to the client or someone else.

143. D: In an ethical dilemma, following one rule means breaking another, so it seems like one cannot make a correct choice no matter which one is chosen. Such dilemmas are unavoidable in social work and in all other helping professions.

144. D: The social worker should always begin with the NASW Code of Ethics when approaching an ethical problem.

145. D: Although tax fraud is a crime, it does not directly physically or emotionally harm others and thus does not require reporting.

146. B: Intelligence might be assumed to be part of competence, and caring underlies all the core values. The sixth core value is the importance of human relationships.

147. C: Confidentiality is usually discussed in the first session, so clients can judge what they will disclose and understand the potential effects of their disclosures.

148. B: The social worker should first try to have the order rescinded, then try to limit the information and ask the court to seal the file, and when every other possibility has been attempted, along with any efforts to prevent or ameliorate harm to the client, provide the information.

149. D: A subpoena does not require the social worker to comply, only to respond to the notice. Records do not have to be supplied until ordered by the court.

150. C: The media should not gain access to confidential client records.

151. B: A social worker cannot control how members of a family or group will use confidential information. In fact, if people come to group work because of familial or social conflicts, violating group confidentiality is just one of the ways members can express conflict and reenact betrayals from life outside the group.

152. C: Clients have the right to access their records. If something in the record is likely to cause harm to the client, the social worker can deny the client's access or may choose to open the record with the client, to work through the information, and address any conflicts together.

153. C: The rights of parents or guardians to access and release minors' confidential records are allocated (or prevented) and upheld by the law. If a disagreement arises about the social worker's decision to give parents access, it can only be effectively conducted through legal channels. To protect the client and to act legally as well as ethically, the social worker must clearly understand the legalities of this situation.

154. D: If the client's right to self-determination means making mistakes, the social worker has to allow the client the freedom to act. Only when the client's actions will bring about serious risk to him- or herself or someone else must the social worker take action to limit the client's freedom.

155. A: Informing the client as much as possible as to his or her rights and of possible treatment risks is an ethical approach, but it would be foolhardy, unethical, and potentially legally actionable to "promise" anything, much less the resolution of problems. For one thing, much of what happens in social work remains the decision of the client and the outcome of his or her activities.

156. D: Consent to disclosure is required unless harm to the client or others is imminent or if the social worker is being sued by the client and needs to use the records in self-defense.

157. A: Even clients who may not have the cognitive or functional skills to make informed decisions should be asked about their wishes, and efforts should be made to accommodate them. Disability does not mean a person forfeits self-determination: To the extent they are able, they should be supported in making choices in their happiness.

158. C: Laws regarding the emancipation of minors (age limits, conditions under which they may be granted emancipated status, etc.) are unique to and regulated by, each state.

159. C: Permanency planning is based on the belief that a child's original home is the best place, because children need stability. The idea is to make the home safe and caring by working with the caregivers, rather than to remove the child.

160. B: The WHODAS will give Fran a reliable and valid measure of Lisa's abilities and provide Fran with documentation should she need to apply for additional help on her client's behalf.

161. D: Until the client is legally judged incompetent, the social worker may assume competence.

162. B: Protecting client privacy and giving the client information necessary for clients to make decisions about their well-being are two ways social workers support clients' right to self-determination.

163. A: When clients make decisions that are likely to harm themselves or others, social workers have a duty to prevent harm whenever possible. Also, laws mandating reporting of abuse and other antisocial acts provide social workers with options for acting to limit clients' freedom to commit various crimes.

164. C: In empathy, the social worker places him- or herself firmly on the client's side, acting supportively, working to understand the client's experience, and establishing a trusting and stable relationship.

165. B: In transference, the client unconsciously projects feelings and ideas from other important relationships onto the helper and then acts as if the projections are true. The client isn't aware of having done that, and an important part of Freudian analysis is for the therapist to bring those unconscious projections into the client's conscious and interpret them, freeing the client from the transference.

166. C: The social worker accepts the client as well as giving the client feedback that isn't tainted by an emotional investment on the part of the social worker; rather, the feedback is positive, authentic, and caring.

167. D: Inappropriate self-disclosure may occur when a social worker is unconsciously trying to work out his or her own issues, which is a boundary violation because it is not being done in the best interests of the client.

168. C: In secondary trauma, the helper loses the emotional distance needed to remain safe from reacting to a client's traumatic experiences. Supportive supervision and dedicated self-care are two ways to help social workers whose clients have been traumatized and who are likely at some point to become overwhelmed with the client's suffering.

169. D: Parallel process is a particular subtype of countertransference, in which the process of therapist and client becomes unintentionally reenacted between the therapist and his or her supervisor. Countertransference plays itself out in many different ways, but parallel process is especially unnerving (or delightful, depending on your viewpoint) because the supervisor and therapist unconsciously recapitulate a feature of the client-therapist relationship: It's almost like "channeling," and when it is caught early and properly interpreted, it can be a powerful agent of potential change.

170. C: The most important goal is to help clients: Evaluations that help social workers improve, that support them in their professional work and advancement, and that give them encouragement as well as honest, constructive feedback will ultimately benefit clients.

Secret Key #1 - Time is Your Greatest Enemy

Pace Yourself

Wear a watch. At the beginning of the test, check the time (or start a chronometer on your watch to count the minutes), and check the time after every few questions to make sure you are "on schedule."

If you are forced to speed up, do it efficiently. Usually one or more answer choices can be eliminated without too much difficulty. Above all, don't panic. Don't speed up and just begin guessing at random choices. By pacing yourself, and continually monitoring your progress against your watch, you will always know exactly how far ahead or behind you are with your available time. If you find that you are one minute behind on the test, don't skip one question without spending any time on it, just to catch back up. Take 15 fewer seconds on the next four questions, and after four questions you'll have caught back up. Once you catch back up, you can continue working each problem at your normal pace.

Furthermore, don't dwell on the problems that you were rushed on. If a problem was taking up too much time and you made a hurried guess, it must be difficult. The difficult questions are the ones you are most likely to miss anyway, so it isn't a big loss. It is better to end with more time than you need than to run out of time.

Lastly, sometimes it is beneficial to slow down if you are constantly getting ahead of time. You are always more likely to catch a careless mistake by working more slowly than quickly, and among very high-scoring test takers (those who are likely to have lots of time left over), careless errors affect the score more than mastery of material.

Secret Key #2 - Guessing is not Guesswork

You probably know that guessing is a good idea. Unlike other standardized tests, there is no penalty for getting a wrong answer. Even if you have no idea about a question, you still have a 20-25% chance of getting it right.

Most test takers do not understand the impact that proper guessing can have on their score. Unless you score extremely high, guessing will significantly contribute to your final score.

Monkeys Take the Test

What most test takers don't realize is that to insure that 20-25% chance, you have to guess randomly. If you put 20 monkeys in a room to take this test, assuming they answered once per question and behaved themselves, on average they would get 20-25% of the questions correct. Put 20 test takers in the room, and the average will be much lower among guessed questions. Why?
1. The test writers intentionally write deceptive answer choices that "look" right. A test taker has no idea about a question, so he picks the "best looking" answer, which is often wrong. The monkey has no idea what looks good and what doesn't, so it will consistently be right about 20-25% of the time.
2. Test takers will eliminate answer choices from the guessing pool based on a hunch or intuition. Simple but correct answers often get excluded, leaving a 0% chance of being correct. The monkey has no clue, and often gets lucky with the best choice.

This is why the process of elimination endorsed by most test courses is flawed and detrimental to your performance. Test takers don't guess; they make an ignorant stab in the dark that is usually worse than random.

$5 Challenge

Let me introduce one of the most valuable ideas of this course—the $5 challenge:

You only mark your "best guess" if you are willing to bet $5 on it.
You only eliminate choices from guessing if you are willing to bet $5 on it.

Why $5? Five dollars is an amount of money that is small yet not insignificant, and can really add up fast (20 questions could cost you $100). Likewise, each answer choice on one question of the test will have a small impact on your overall score, but it can really add up to a lot of points in the end.

The process of elimination IS valuable. The following shows your chance of guessing it right:

If you eliminate wrong answer choices until only this many remain:	Chance of getting it correct:
1	100%
2	50%
3	33%

However, if you accidentally eliminate the right answer or go on a hunch for an incorrect answer, your chances drop dramatically—to 0%. By guessing among all the answer choices, you are GUARANTEED to have a shot at the right answer.

That's why the $5 test is so valuable. If you give up the advantage and safety of a pure guess, it had better be worth the risk.

What we still haven't covered is how to be sure that whatever guess you make is truly random. Here's the easiest way:

Always pick the first answer choice among those remaining.

Such a technique means that you have decided, **before you see a single test question**, exactly how you are going to guess, and since the order of choices tells you nothing about which one is correct, this guessing technique is perfectly random.

This section is not meant to scare you away from making educated guesses or eliminating choices; you just need to define when a choice is worth eliminating. The $5 test, along with a pre-defined random guessing strategy, is the best way to make sure you reap all of the benefits of guessing.

Secret Key #3 - Practice Smarter, Not Harder

Many test takers delay the test preparation process because they dread the awful amounts of practice time they think necessary to succeed on the test. We have refined an effective method that will take you only a fraction of the time.

There are a number of "obstacles" in the path to success. Among these are answering questions, finishing in time, and mastering test-taking strategies. All must be executed on the day of the test at peak performance, or your score will suffer. The test is a mental marathon that has a large impact on your future.

Just like a marathon runner, it is important to work your way up to the full challenge. So first you just worry about questions, and then time, and finally strategy:

Success Strategy

1. Find a good source for practice tests.
2. If you are willing to make a larger time investment, consider using more than one study guide. Often the different approaches of multiple authors will help you "get" difficult concepts.
3. Take a practice test with no time constraints, with all study helps, "open book." Take your time with questions and focus on applying strategies.
4. Take a practice test with time constraints, with all guides, "open book."
5. Take a final practice test without open material and with time limits.

If you have time to take more practice tests, just repeat step 5. By gradually exposing yourself to the full rigors of the test environment, you will condition your mind to the stress of test day and maximize your success.

Secret Key #4 - Prepare, Don't Procrastinate

Let me state an obvious fact: if you take the test three times, you will probably get three different scores. This is due to the way you feel on test day, the level of preparedness you have, and the version of the test you see. Despite the test writers' claims to the contrary, some versions of the test WILL be easier for you than others.

Since your future depends so much on your score, you should maximize your chances of success. In order to maximize the likelihood of success, you've got to prepare in advance. This means taking practice tests and spending time learning the information and test taking strategies you will need to succeed.

Never go take the actual test as a "practice" test, expecting that you can just take it again if you need to. Take all the practice tests you can on your own, but when you go to take the official test, be prepared, be focused, and do your best the first time!

Secret Key #5 - Test Yourself

Everyone knows that time is money. There is no need to spend too much of your time or too little of your time preparing for the test. You should only spend as much of your precious time preparing as is necessary for you to get the score you need.

Once you have taken a practice test under real conditions of time constraints, then you will know if you are ready for the test or not.

If you have scored extremely high the first time that you take the practice test, then there is not much point in spending countless hours studying. You are already there.

Benchmark your abilities by retaking practice tests and seeing how much you have improved. Once you consistently score high enough to guarantee success, then you are ready.

If you have scored well below where you need, then knuckle down and begin studying in earnest. Check your improvement regularly through the use of practice tests under real conditions. Above all, don't worry, panic, or give up. The key is perseverance!

Then, when you go to take the test, remain confident and remember how well you did on the practice tests. If you can score high enough on a practice test, then you can do the same on the real thing.

General Strategies

The most important thing you can do is to ignore your fears and jump into the test immediately. Do not be overwhelmed by any strange-sounding terms. You have to jump into the test like jumping into a pool—all at once is the easiest way.

Make Predictions

As you read and understand the question, try to guess what the answer will be. Remember that several of the answer choices are wrong, and once you begin reading them, your mind will immediately become cluttered with answer choices designed to throw you off. Your mind is typically the most focused immediately after you have read the question and digested its contents. If you can, try to predict what the correct answer will be. You may be surprised at what you can predict.

Quickly scan the choices and see if your prediction is in the listed answer choices. If it is, then you can be quite confident that you have the right answer. It still won't hurt to check the other answer choices, but most of the time, you've got it!

Answer the Question

It may seem obvious to only pick answer choices that answer the question, but the test writers can create some excellent answer choices that are wrong. Don't pick an answer just because it sounds right, or you believe it to be true. It MUST answer the question. Once you've made your selection, always go back and check it against the question and make sure that you didn't misread the question and that the answer choice does answer the question posed.

Benchmark

After you read the first answer choice, decide if you think it sounds correct or not. If it doesn't, move on to the next answer choice. If it does, mentally mark that answer choice. This doesn't mean that you've definitely selected it as your answer choice, it just means that it's the best you've seen thus far. Go ahead and read the next choice. If the next choice is worse than the one you've already selected, keep going to the next answer choice. If the next choice is better than the choice you've already selected, mentally mark the new answer choice as your best guess.

The first answer choice that you select becomes your standard. Every other answer choice must be benchmarked against that standard. That choice is correct until proven otherwise by another answer choice beating it out. Once you've decided that no other answer choice seems as good, do one final check to ensure that your answer choice answers the question posed.

Valid Information

Don't discount any of the information provided in the question. Every piece of information may be necessary to determine the correct answer. None of the information in the question is there to throw you off (while the answer choices will certainly have information to throw you off). If two seemingly unrelated topics are discussed, don't ignore either. You can be confident there is a relationship, or it wouldn't be included in the question, and you are probably going to have to determine what is that relationship to find the answer.

Avoid "Fact Traps"

Don't get distracted by a choice that is factually true. Your search is for the answer that answers the question. Stay focused and don't fall for an answer that is true but irrelevant. Always go back to the question and make sure you're choosing an answer that actually answers the question and is not just a true statement. An answer can be factually correct, but it MUST answer the question asked. Additionally, two answers can both be seemingly correct, so be sure to read all of the answer choices, and make sure that you get the one that BEST answers the question.

Milk the Question

Some of the questions may throw you completely off. They might deal with a subject you have not been exposed to, or one that you haven't reviewed in years. While your lack of knowledge about the subject will be a hindrance, the question itself can give you many clues that will help you find the correct answer. Read the question carefully and look for clues. Watch particularly for adjectives and nouns describing difficult terms or words that you don't recognize. Regardless of whether you completely understand a word or not, replacing it with a synonym, either provided or one you more familiar with, may help you to understand what the questions are asking. Rather than wracking your mind about specific detailed information concerning a difficult term or word, try to use mental substitutes that are easier to understand.

The Trap of Familiarity

Don't just choose a word because you recognize it. On difficult questions, you may not recognize a number of words in the answer choices. The test writers don't put "make-believe" words on the test, so don't think that just because you only recognize all the words in one answer choice that that answer choice must be correct. If you only recognize words in one answer choice, then focus on that one. Is it correct? Try your best to determine if it is correct. If it is, that's great. If not, eliminate it. Each word and answer choice you eliminate increases your chances of getting the question correct, even if you then have to guess among the unfamiliar choices.

Eliminate Answers

Eliminate choices as soon as you realize they are wrong. But be careful! Make sure you consider all of the possible answer choices. Just because one appears right, doesn't mean that the next one won't be even better! The test writers will usually put more than one good answer choice for every question, so read all of them. Don't worry if you are stuck between two that seem right. By getting down to just two remaining possible choices, your odds are now 50/50. Rather than wasting too much time, play the odds. You are guessing, but guessing wisely because you've been able to knock out some of the answer choices that you know are wrong. If you are eliminating choices and realize that the last answer choice you are left with is also obviously wrong, don't panic. Start over and consider each choice again. There may easily be something that you missed the first time and will realize on the second pass.

Tough Questions

If you are stumped on a problem or it appears too hard or too difficult, don't waste time. Move on! Remember though, if you can quickly check for obviously incorrect answer choices, your chances of guessing correctly are greatly improved. Before you completely give up, at least try to knock out a couple of possible answers. Eliminate what you can and then guess at the remaining answer choices before moving on.

Brainstorm

If you get stuck on a difficult question, spend a few seconds quickly brainstorming. Run through the complete list of possible answer choices. Look at each choice and ask yourself, "Could this answer the question satisfactorily?" Go through each answer choice and consider it independently of the others. By systematically going through all possibilities, you may find something that you would otherwise overlook. Remember though that when you get stuck, it's important to try to keep moving.

Read Carefully

Understand the problem. Read the question and answer choices carefully. Don't miss the question because you misread the terms. You have plenty of time to read each question thoroughly and make sure you understand what is being asked. Yet a happy medium must be attained, so don't waste too much time. You must read carefully, but efficiently.

Face Value

When in doubt, use common sense. Always accept the situation in the problem at face value. Don't read too much into it. These problems will not require you to make huge leaps of logic. The test writers aren't trying to throw you off with a cheap trick. If you have to go beyond creativity and make a leap of logic in order to have an answer choice answer the question, then you should look at the other answer choices. Don't overcomplicate the problem by creating theoretical relationships or explanations that will warp time or space. These are normal problems rooted in reality. It's just that the applicable relationship or explanation may not be readily apparent and you have to figure things out. Use your common sense to interpret anything that isn't clear.

Prefixes

If you're having trouble with a word in the question or answer choices, try dissecting it. Take advantage of every clue that the word might include. Prefixes and suffixes can be a huge help. Usually they allow you to determine a basic meaning. Pre- means before, post- means after, pro - is positive, de- is negative. From these prefixes and suffixes, you can get an idea of the general meaning of the word and try to put it into context. Beware though of any traps. Just because con- is the opposite of pro-, doesn't necessarily mean congress is the opposite of progress!

Hedge Phrases

Watch out for critical hedge phrases, led off with words such as "likely," "may," "can," "sometimes," "often," "almost," "mostly," "usually," "generally," "rarely," and "sometimes." Question writers insert these hedge phrases to cover every possibility. Often an answer choice will be wrong simply because it leaves no room for exception. Unless the situation calls for them, avoid answer choices that have definitive words like "exactly," and "always."

Switchback Words

Stay alert for "switchbacks." These are the words and phrases frequently used to alert you to shifts in thought. The most common switchback word is "but." Others include "although," "however," "nevertheless," "on the other hand," "even though," "while," "in spite of," "despite," and "regardless of."

New Information

Correct answer choices will rarely have completely new information included. Answer choices typically are straightforward reflections of the material asked about and will directly relate to the question. If a new piece of information is included in an answer choice that doesn't even seem to relate to the topic being asked about, then that answer choice is likely incorrect. All of the information needed to answer the question is usually provided for you in the question. You should not have to make guesses that are unsupported or choose answer choices that require unknown information that cannot be reasoned from what is given.

Time Management

On technical questions, don't get lost on the technical terms. Don't spend too much time on any one question. If you don't know what a term means, then odds are you aren't going to get much further since you don't have a dictionary. You should be able to immediately recognize whether or not you know a term. If you don't, work with the other clues that you have—the other answer choices and terms provided—but don't waste too much time trying to figure out a difficult term that you don't know.

Contextual Clues

Look for contextual clues. An answer can be right but not the correct answer. The contextual clues will help you find the answer that is most right and is correct. Understand the context in which a phrase or statement is made. This will help you make important distinctions.

Don't Panic

Panicking will not answer any questions for you; therefore, it isn't helpful. When you first see the question, if your mind goes blank, take a deep breath. Force yourself to mechanically go through the steps of solving the problem using the strategies you've learned.

Pace Yourself

Don't get clock fever. It's easy to be overwhelmed when you're looking at a page full of questions, your mind is full of random thoughts and feeling confused, and the clock is ticking down faster than you would like. Calm down and maintain the pace that you have set for yourself. As long as you are on track by monitoring your pace, you are guaranteed to have enough time for yourself. When you get to the last few minutes of the test, it may seem like you won't have enough time left, but if you only have as many questions as you should have left at that point, then you're right on track!

Answer Selection

The best way to pick an answer choice is to eliminate all of those that are wrong, until only one is left and confirm that is the correct answer. Sometimes though, an answer choice may immediately look right. Be careful! Take a second to make sure that the other choices are not equally obvious. Don't make a hasty mistake. There are only two times that you should stop before checking other answers. First is when you are positive that the answer choice you have selected is correct. Second is when time is almost out and you have to make a quick guess!

Check Your Work

Since you will probably not know every term listed and the answer to every question, it is important that you get credit for the ones that you do know. Don't miss any questions through careless mistakes. If at all possible, try to take a second to look back over your answer selection and make sure you've selected the correct answer choice and haven't made a costly careless mistake (such as marking an answer choice that you didn't mean to mark). The time it takes for this quick double check should more than pay for itself in caught mistakes.

Beware of Directly Quoted Answers

Sometimes an answer choice will repeat word for word a portion of the question or reference section. However, beware of such exact duplication. It may be a trap! More than likely, the correct choice will paraphrase or summarize a point, rather than being exactly the same wording.

Slang

Scientific sounding answers are better than slang ones. An answer choice that begins "To compare the outcomes..." is much more likely to be correct than one that begins "Because some people insisted..."

Extreme Statements

Avoid wild answers that throw out highly controversial ideas that are proclaimed as established fact. An answer choice that states the "process should used in certain situations, if..." is much more likely to be correct than one that states the "process should be discontinued completely." The first is a calm rational statement and doesn't even make a definitive, uncompromising stance, using a hedge word "if" to provide wiggle room, whereas the second choice is a radical idea and far more extreme.

Answer Choice Families

When you have two or more answer choices that are direct opposites or parallels, one of them is usually the correct answer. For instance, if one answer choice states "x increases" and another answer choice states "x decreases" or "y increases," then those two or three answer choices are very similar in construction and fall into the same family of answer choices. A family of answer choices consists of two or three answer choices, very similar in construction, but often with directly opposite meanings. Usually the correct answer choice will be in that family of answer choices. The "odd man out" or answer choice that doesn't seem to fit the parallel construction of the other answer choices is more likely to be incorrect.

Special Report: How to Overcome Test Anxiety

The very nature of tests caters to some level of anxiety, nervousness, or tension, just as we feel for any important event that occurs in our lives. A little bit of anxiety or nervousness can be a good thing. It helps us with motivation, and makes achievement just that much sweeter. However, too much anxiety can be a problem, especially if it hinders our ability to function and perform.

"Test anxiety," is the term that refers to the emotional reactions that some test-takers experience when faced with a test or exam. Having a fear of testing and exams is based upon a rational fear, since the test-taker's performance can shape the course of an academic career. Nevertheless, experiencing excessive fear of examinations will only interfere with the test-taker's ability to perform and chance to be successful.

There are a large variety of causes that can contribute to the development and sensation of test anxiety. These include, but are not limited to, lack of preparation and worrying about issues surrounding the test.

Lack of Preparation

Lack of preparation can be identified by the following behaviors or situations:

Not scheduling enough time to study, and therefore cramming the night before the test or exam
Managing time poorly, to create the sensation that there is not enough time to do everything
Failing to organize the text information in advance, so that the study material consists of the entire text and not simply the pertinent information
Poor overall studying habits

Worrying, on the other hand, can be related to both the test taker, or many other factors around him/her that will be affected by the results of the test. These include worrying about:

Previous performances on similar exams, or exams in general
How friends and other students are achieving
The negative consequences that will result from a poor grade or failure

There are three primary elements to test anxiety. Physical components, which involve the same typical bodily reactions as those to acute anxiety (to be discussed below). Emotional factors have to do with fear or panic. Mental or cognitive issues concerning attention spans and memory abilities.

Physical Signals

There are many different symptoms of test anxiety, and these are not limited to mental and emotional strain. Frequently there are a range of physical signals that will let a test taker know that he/she is suffering from test anxiety. These bodily changes can include the following:

Perspiring
Sweaty palms
Wet, trembling hands
Nausea
Dry mouth
A knot in the stomach
Headache
Faintness
Muscle tension
Aching shoulders, back and neck
Rapid heart beat
Feeling too hot/cold

To recognize the sensation of test anxiety, a test-taker should monitor him/herself for the following sensations:

The physical distress symptoms as listed above
Emotional sensitivity, expressing emotional feelings such as the need to cry or laugh too much, or a sensation of anger or helplessness
A decreased ability to think, causing the test-taker to blank out or have racing thoughts that are hard to organize or control.

Though most students will feel some level of anxiety when faced with a test or exam, the majority can cope with that anxiety and maintain it at a manageable level. However, those who cannot are faced with a very real and very serious condition, which can and should be controlled for the immeasurable benefit of this sufferer.

Naturally, these sensations lead to negative results for the testing experience. The most common effects of test anxiety have to do with nervousness and mental blocking.

Nervousness

Nervousness can appear in several different levels:

The test-taker's difficulty, or even inability to read and understand the questions on the test
The difficulty or inability to organize thoughts to a coherent form
The difficulty or inability to recall key words and concepts relating to the testing questions (especially essays)
The receipt of poor grades on a test, though the test material was well known by the test taker

Conversely, a person may also experience mental blocking, which involves:

Blanking out on test questions
Only remembering the correct answers to the questions when the test has already finished.

Fortunately for test anxiety sufferers, beating these feelings, to a large degree, has to do with proper preparation. When a test taker has a feeling of preparedness, then anxiety will be dramatically lessened.

The first step to resolving anxiety issues is to distinguish which of the two types of anxiety are being suffered. If the anxiety is a direct result of a lack of preparation, this should be considered a normal reaction, and the anxiety level (as opposed to the test results) shouldn't be anything to worry about. However, if, when adequately prepared, the test-taker still panics, blanks out, or seems to overreact, this is not a fully rational reaction. While this can be considered normal too, there are many ways to combat and overcome these effects.

Remember that anxiety cannot be entirely eliminated, however, there are ways to minimize it, to make the anxiety easier to manage. Preparation is one of the best ways to minimize test anxiety. Therefore the following techniques are wise in order to best fight off any anxiety that may want to build.

To begin with, try to avoid cramming before a test, whenever it is possible. By trying to memorize an entire term's worth of information in one day, you'll be shocking your system, and not giving yourself a very good chance to absorb the information. This is an easy path to anxiety, so for those who suffer from test anxiety, cramming should not even be considered an option.

Instead of cramming, work throughout the semester to combine all of the material which is presented throughout the semester, and work on it gradually as the course goes by, making sure to master the main concepts first, leaving minor details for a week or so before the test.

To study for the upcoming exam, be sure to pose questions that may be on the examination, to gauge the ability to answer them by integrating the ideas from your texts, notes and lectures, as well as any supplementary readings.

If it is truly impossible to cover all of the information that was covered in that particular term, concentrate on the most important portions, that can be covered very well. Learn these concepts as best as possible, so that when the test comes, a goal can be made to use these concepts as presentations of your knowledge.

In addition to study habits, changes in attitude are critical to beating a struggle with test anxiety. In fact, an improvement of the perspective over the entire test-taking experience can actually help a test taker to enjoy studying and therefore improve the overall experience. Be certain not to overemphasize the significance of the grade - know that the result of the test is neither a reflection of self worth, nor is it a measure of intelligence; one grade will not predict a person's future success.

To improve an overall testing outlook, the following steps should be tried:

Keeping in mind that the most reasonable expectation for taking a test is to expect to try to demonstrate as much of what you know as you possibly can.

Reminding ourselves that a test is only one test; this is not the only one, and there will be others.

The thought of thinking of oneself in an irrational, all-or-nothing term should be avoided at all costs.

A reward should be designated for after the test, so there's something to look forward to. Whether it be going to a movie, going out to eat, or simply visiting friends, schedule it in advance, and do it no matter what result is expected on the exam.

Test-takers should also keep in mind that the basics are some of the most important things, even beyond anti-anxiety techniques and studying. Never neglect the basic social, emotional and biological needs, in order to try to absorb information. In order to best achieve, these three factors must be held as just as important as the studying itself.

Study Steps

Remember the following important steps for studying:

Maintain healthy nutrition and exercise habits. Continue both your recreational activities and social pass times. These both contribute to your physical and emotional well being.
Be certain to get a good amount of sleep, especially the night before the test, because when you're overtired you are not able to perform to the best of your best ability.
Keep the studying pace to a moderate level by taking breaks when they are needed, and varying the work whenever possible, to keep the mind fresh instead of getting bored.
When enough studying has been done that all the material that can be learned has been learned, and the test taker is prepared for the test, stop studying and do something relaxing such as listening to music, watching a movie, or taking a warm bubble bath.

There are also many other techniques to minimize the uneasiness or apprehension that is experienced along with test anxiety before, during, or even after the examination. In fact, there are a great deal of things that can be done to stop anxiety from interfering with lifestyle and performance. Again, remember that anxiety will not be eliminated entirely, and it shouldn't be. Otherwise that "up" feeling for exams would not exist, and most of us depend on that sensation to perform better than usual. However, this anxiety has to be at a level that is manageable.

Of course, as we have just discussed, being prepared for the exam is half the battle right away. Attending all classes, finding out what knowledge will be expected on the exam, and knowing the exam schedules are easy steps to lowering anxiety. Keeping up with work will remove the need to cram, and efficient study habits will eliminate wasted time. Studying should be done in an ideal location for concentration, so that it is simple to become interested in the material and give it complete attention. A method such as SQ3R (Survey, Question, Read, Recite, Review) is a wonderful key to follow to make sure that the study habits are as effective as possible, especially in the case of learning from a textbook. Flashcards are great techniques for memorization. Learning to take good notes will mean that notes will be full of useful information, so that less sifting will need to be done to seek out what is pertinent for studying. Reviewing notes after class and then again on occasion will keep the information fresh in the mind. From notes that have been taken summary sheets and outlines can be made for simpler reviewing.

A study group can also be a very motivational and helpful place to study, as there will be a sharing of ideas, all of the minds can work together, to make sure that everyone understands, and the studying will be made more interesting because it will be a social occasion.

Basically, though, as long as the test-taker remains organized and self confident, with efficient study habits, less time will need to be spent studying, and higher grades will be achieved.

To become self confident, there are many useful steps. The first of these is "self talk." It has been shown through extensive research, that self-talk for students who suffer from test anxiety, should be well monitored, in order to make sure that it contributes to self confidence as opposed to sinking the student. Frequently the self talk of test-anxious students is negative or self-defeating, thinking that everyone else is smarter and faster, that they always mess up, and that if they don't do well, they'll fail the entire course. It is important to decreasing anxiety that awareness is made of self talk. Try writing any negative self thoughts and then disputing them with a positive statement instead. Begin self-encouragement as though it was a friend speaking. Repeat positive statements to help reprogram the mind to believing in successes instead of failures.

Helpful Techniques

Other extremely helpful techniques include:

Self-visualization of doing well and reaching goals
While aiming for an "A" level of understanding, don't try to "overprotect" by setting your expectations lower. This will only convince the mind to stop studying in order to meet the lower expectations.
Don't make comparisons with the results or habits of other students. These are individual factors, and different things work for different people, causing different results.
Strive to become an expert in learning what works well, and what can be done in order to improve. Consider collecting this data in a journal.
Create rewards for after studying instead of doing things before studying that will only turn into avoidance behaviors.
Make a practice of relaxing - by using methods such as progressive relaxation, self-hypnosis, guided imagery, etc - in order to make relaxation an automatic sensation.
Work on creating a state of relaxed concentration so that concentrating will take on the focus of the mind, so that none will be wasted on worrying.
Take good care of the physical self by eating well and getting enough sleep.
Plan in time for exercise and stick to this plan.

Beyond these techniques, there are other methods to be used before, during and after the test that will help the test-taker perform well in addition to overcoming anxiety.

Before the exam comes the academic preparation. This involves establishing a study schedule and beginning at least one week before the actual date of the test. By doing this, the anxiety of not having enough time to study for the test will be automatically eliminated. Moreover, this will make the studying a much more effective experience, ensuring that the learning will be an easier process. This relieves much undue pressure on the test-taker.

Summary sheets, note cards, and flash cards with the main concepts and examples of these main concepts should be prepared in advance of the actual studying time. A topic should never be eliminated from this process. By omitting a topic because it isn't expected to be on the test is only setting up the test-taker for anxiety should it actually appear on the exam. Utilize the course syllabus for laying out the topics that should be studied. Carefully go over the notes that were made in class, paying special attention to any of the issues that the professor took special care to emphasize while lecturing in class. In the textbooks, use the chapter review, or if possible, the chapter tests, to begin your review.

It may even be possible to ask the instructor what information will be covered on the exam, or what the format of the exam will be (for example, multiple choice, essay, free form, true-false). Additionally, see if it is possible to find out how many questions will be on the test. If a review sheet or sample test has been offered by the professor, make good use of it, above anything else, for the preparation for the test. Another great resource for getting to know the examination is reviewing tests from previous semesters. Use these tests to review, and aim to achieve a 100% score on each of the possible topics. With a few exceptions, the goal that you set for yourself is the highest one that you will reach.

Take all of the questions that were assigned as homework, and rework them to any other possible course material. The more problems reworked, the more skill and confidence will form as a result. When forming the solution to a problem, write out each of the steps. Don't simply do head work. By doing as many steps on paper as possible, much clarification and therefore confidence will be formed. Do this with as many homework problems as possible, before checking the answers. By checking the answer after each problem, a reinforcement will exist, that will not be on the exam. Study situations should be as exam-like as possible, to prime the test-taker's system for the experience. By waiting to check the answers at the end, a psychological advantage will be formed, to decrease the stress factor.

Another fantastic reason for not cramming is the avoidance of confusion in concepts, especially when it comes to mathematics. 8-10 hours of study will become one hundred percent more effective if it is spread out over a week or at least several days, instead of doing it all in one sitting. Recognize that the human brain requires time in order to assimilate new material, so frequent breaks and a span of study time over several days will be much more beneficial.

Additionally, don't study right up until the point of the exam. Studying should stop a minimum of one hour before the exam begins. This allows the brain to rest and put things in their proper order. This will also provide the time to become as relaxed as possible when going into the examination room. The test-taker will also have time to eat well and eat sensibly. Know that the brain needs food as much as the rest of the body. With enough food and enough sleep, as well as a relaxed attitude, the body and the mind are primed for success.

Avoid any anxious classmates who are talking about the exam. These students only spread anxiety, and are not worth sharing the anxious sentimentalities.

Before the test also involves creating a positive attitude, so mental preparation should also be a point of concentration. There are many keys to creating a positive attitude. Should fears become rushing in, make a visualization of taking the exam, doing well, and seeing an A written on the paper. Write out a list of affirmations that will bring a feeling of confidence, such as "I am doing well in my English class," "I studied well and know my material," "I enjoy this class." Even if the affirmations aren't believed at first, it sends a positive message to the subconscious which will result in an alteration of the overall belief system, which is the system that creates reality.

If a sensation of panic begins, work with the fear and imagine the very worst! Work through the entire scenario of not passing the test, failing the entire course, and dropping out of school, followed by not getting a job, and pushing a shopping cart through the dark alley where you'll live. This will place things into perspective! Then, practice deep breathing and create a visualization of the opposite situation - achieving an "A" on the exam, passing the entire course, receiving the degree at a graduation ceremony.

On the day of the test, there are many things to be done to ensure the best results, as well as the most calm outlook. The following stages are suggested in order to maximize test-taking potential:

Begin the examination day with a moderate breakfast, and avoid any coffee or beverages with caffeine if the test taker is prone to jitters. Even people who are used to managing caffeine can feel jittery or light-headed when it is taken on a test day.
Attempt to do something that is relaxing before the examination begins. As last minute cramming clouds the mastering of overall concepts, it is better to use this time to create a calming outlook.
Be certain to arrive at the test location well in advance, in order to provide time to select a location that is away from doors, windows and other distractions, as well as giving enough time to relax before the test begins.
Keep away from anxiety generating classmates who will upset the sensation of stability and relaxation that is being attempted before the exam.
Should the waiting period before the exam begins cause anxiety, create a self-distraction by reading a light magazine or something else that is relaxing and simple.

During the exam itself, read the entire exam from beginning to end, and find out how much time should be allotted to each individual problem. Once writing the exam, should more time be taken for a problem, it should be abandoned, in order to begin another problem. If there is time at the end, the unfinished problem can always be returned to and completed.

Read the instructions very carefully - twice - so that unpleasant surprises won't follow during or after the exam has ended.

When writing the exam, pretend that the situation is actually simply the completion of homework within a library, or at home. This will assist in forming a relaxed atmosphere, and will allow the brain extra focus for the complex thinking function.

Begin the exam with all of the questions with which the most confidence is felt. This will build the confidence level regarding the entire exam and will begin a quality momentum. This will also create encouragement for trying the problems where uncertainty resides.

Going with the "gut instinct" is always the way to go when solving a problem. Second guessing should be avoided at all costs. Have confidence in the ability to do well.

For essay questions, create an outline in advance that will keep the mind organized and make certain that all of the points are remembered. For multiple choice, read every answer, even if the correct one has been spotted - a better one may exist.

Continue at a pace that is reasonable and not rushed, in order to be able to work carefully. Provide enough time to go over the answers at the end, to check for small errors that can be corrected.

Should a feeling of panic begin, breathe deeply, and think of the feeling of the body releasing sand through its pores. Visualize a calm, peaceful place, and include all of the sights, sounds and sensations of this image. Continue the deep breathing, and take a few minutes to continue this with closed eyes. When all is well again, return to the test.

If a "blanking" occurs for a certain question, skip it and move on to the next question. There will be time to return to the other question later. Get everything done that can be done, first, to guarantee all the grades that can be compiled, and to build all of the confidence possible. Then return to the weaker questions to build the marks from there.

Remember, one's own reality can be created, so as long as the belief is there, success will follow. And remember: anxiety can happen later, right now, there's an exam to be written!

After the examination is complete, whether there is a feeling for a good grade or a bad grade, don't dwell on the exam, and be certain to follow through on the reward that was promised...and enjoy it! Don't dwell on any mistakes that have been made, as there is nothing that can be done at this point anyway.

Additionally, don't begin to study for the next test right away. Do something relaxing for a while, and let the mind relax and prepare itself to begin absorbing information again.

From the results of the exam - both the grade and the entire experience, be certain to learn from what has gone on. Perfect studying habits and work some more on confidence in order to make the next examination experience even better than the last one.

Learn to avoid places where openings occurred for laziness, procrastination and day dreaming.

Use the time between this exam and the next one to better learn to relax, even learning to relax on cue, so that any anxiety can be controlled during the next exam. Learn how to relax the body. Slouch in your chair if that helps. Tighten and then relax all of the different muscle groups, one group at a time, beginning with the feet and then working all the way up to the neck and face. This will ultimately relax the muscles more than they were to begin with. Learn how to breathe deeply and comfortably, and focus on this breathing going in and out as a relaxing thought. With every exhale, repeat the word "relax."

As common as test anxiety is, it is very possible to overcome it. Make yourself one of the test-takers who overcome this frustrating hindrance.

Additional Bonus Material

Due to our efforts to try to keep this book to a manageable length, we've created a link that will give you access to all of your additional bonus material.

Please visit http://www.mometrix.com/bonus948/aswbbachelors to access the information.

CPSIA information can be obtained
at www.ICGtesting.com
Printed in the USA
LVOW09s0615240518
578352LV00024B/264/P

9 781609 712174